## DATE DUE

| | |
|---|---|
| | |
| | |
| | |
| | |
| | |
| | |
| | |
| | |
| | |
| | |
| | |
| | |
| | |
| | |
| | |

BRODART, CO.                    Cat. No. 23-221

# About This Book

## Why is this topic important?

Developing our emotional intelligence may be the accomplishment that helps the ship of civilization right itself amid the current storms of chaos. Scientific research has shown that it can increase the profits of organizations that intentionally develop these competencies through all levels of leadership. The stories of thousands of successful coaching clients compellingly attest to the increased meaning, connection, and effectiveness they enjoy in their personal and professional lives as a result of improving their emotional skills and understanding of emotion.

## What can you achieve with this book?

You can learn to help your clients change the way in which they relate to everything that is valuable in their lives. As you help them become increasingly familiar with their emotional control panel and how the dials for each of the strategies and competencies are currently set, they can learn how to change the behaviors and make their lives more effective and satisfying. Without this knowledge, they are left with their faces pressed against the window to the candy store of life simply because they do not know how to open the door. As your clients become more and more successful at connecting with their worlds in the ways that make a meaningful difference, they will naturally model these skills for others, and our evolution will be accelerated.

## How is this book organized?

This book is organized with an introduction and four parts. The Introduction shows how coaching can be matched with emotional intelligence to prevent or repair the emotional rifts, issues, blocks, and catastrophes that undermine our collective mental health and human progress. Part One is composed of two chapters that demonstrate how the competencies of emotional intelligence and the principles for applying them balance to form the perfect foundation for a sound coaching methodology. The second chapter specifically makes the business case for developing emotional intelligence through the coaching process. Part Two contains five chapters specifically designed to teach coaches the five specific strategies that are necessary to help their clients develop emotional and social effectiveness. Part Three, *Developing the Coach,* was contributed by the leaders of Newfield Network as a unique example of the creative methods for developing emotional intelligence they utilize in their coach training program. Part Four includes one chapter of specific examples of how emotional intelligence coaching programs have been used to rebuild emotional effectiveness and team performance in federal agencies such as NASA and one chapter with two more detailed case studies on the application of coaching for emotional intelligence, one is with a team and one with an upwardly mobile executive.

# About Pfeiffer

Pfeiffer serves the professional development and hands-on resource needs of training and human resource practitioners and gives them products to do their jobs better. We deliver proven ideas and solutions from experts in HR development and HR management, and we offer effective and customizable tools to improve workplace performance. From novice to seasoned professional, Pfeiffer is the source you can trust to make yourself and your organization more successful.

**Essential Knowledge** Pfeiffer produces insightful, practical, and comprehensive materials on topics that matter the most to training and HR professionals. Our Essential Knowledge resources translate the expertise of seasoned professionals into practical, how-to guidance on critical workplace issues and problems. These resources are supported by case studies, worksheets, and job aids and are frequently supplemented with CD-ROMs, websites, and other means of making the content easier to read, understand, and use.

**Essential Tools** Pfeiffer's Essential Tools resources save time and expense by offering proven, ready-to-use materials—including exercises, activities, games, instruments, and assessments—for use during a training or-team-learning event. These resources are frequently offered in looseleaf or CD-ROM format to facilitate copying and customization of the material.

Pfeiffer also recognizes the remarkable power of new technologies in expanding the reach and effectiveness of training. While e-hype has often created whizbang solutions in search of a problem, we are dedicated to bringing convenience and enhancements to proven training solutions. All our e-tools comply with rigorous functionality standards. The most appropriate technology wrapped around essential content yields the perfect solution for today's on-the-go trainers and human resource professionals.

**Pfeiffer**
www.pfeiffer.com    *Essential resources for training and HR professionals*

*We dedicate this book to the coaches, coachees, teams,
and organizations throughout the world who commit that
their work and the work of their organizations will help create
sustainable ways to live together on this planet, ways that reduce
human suffering, promote joy, and expand our care for
the precious diversity of life. We fervently advocate for the
application of all practices that can advance humanity's
development of emotional and social intelligence,
twin forms of awareness that reliably lead to peace.*

# A Coach's Guide to Emotional Intelligence

*Strategies for Developing Successful Leaders*

## JAMES BRADFORD TERRELL AND MARCIA HUGHES

*with contributions from Guest Authors*
Julio Olalla,
Terrie Lupberger, and
G. Lee Salmon

Pfeiffer

A Wiley Imprint
www.pfeiffer.com

Published by Pfeiffer
An Imprint of Wiley
989 Market Street, San Francisco, CA 94103-1741

www.pfeiffer.com

For additional copies/bulk purchases of this book in the U.S. please contact 800-274-4434.

Pfeiffer books and products are available through most bookstores. To contact Pfeiffer directly call our Customer Care Department within the U.S. at 800-274-4434, outside the U.S. at 317-572-3985, fax 317-572-4002, or visit www.pfeiffer.com.

Pfeiffer also publishes its books in a variety of electronic formats. Some content that appears in print may not be available in electronic books.

**Library of Congress Cataloging-in-Publication Data**

Hughes, Marcia M.
  A coach's guide to emotional intelligence : strategies for developing successful leaders/Marcia Hughes, James Bradford Terrell.
    p.  cm.
  Includes bibliographical references and index.
  ISBN 978-0-7879-9735-9 (cloth)
  1. Executive coaching.  2. Emotional intelligence.  I. Terrell, James Bradford, 1951-  II. Title.
  HD30.4.H823  2008
  658.4'07124—dc22

                                                                                          2008016487

Acquiring Editor: Lisa Shannon
Director of Development: Kathleen Dolan Davies
Developmental Editor: Janis Chan
Production Editor: Dawn Kilgore

Editor: Rebecca Taff
Editorial Assistant: Marisa Kelley
Manufacturing Supervisor: Becky Morgan

Printed in the United States of America

Printing   10  9  8  7  6  5  4  3  2  1

# Contents

# *Acknowledgments*

The authors wish to acknowledge and thank all of the following people:

The many coaches, coachees, teams, and organizations we have had the great honor to work with. You teach us daily.

Steven Stein, David Groth, Diana Durek, and all our brilliant colleagues at Multi-Health Systems who promote emotional intelligence daily. Reuven Bar-On, Peter Salovey, John D. Mayer, David R. Caruso, Daniel Goleman, Cary Cherniss, Richard E. Boyatzis, and Annie McKee for your pioneering emotional intelligence work.

Martin Delahoussaye, former senior editor at Pfeiffer, for guiding and encouraging us with such good cheer; Lisa Shannon, our helpful editor; Kathleen Davies, director of development; Dawn Kilgore, Pfeiffer production editor; Rebecca Taff; and Michael Snell, our agent, for creating an excellent interface with our publisher and orchestrating a win-win process and continuing down the publishing path with us.

Robert Carkhuff, John Grinder, Richard Bandler, Leslie Lebeau, Judith DeLozier, and Robert Dilts and all their teachers for the phenomenal contributions they have made to our understanding of human communication and how to improve it.

Thomas Lewis, M.D., Fari Amini, M.D., and Richard Lannon, M.D., for writing *A General Theory of Love.* It is one of the most valuable scientific contributions to understanding how we can be better human beings and why that is often such a challenge. The grace and beauty of its elegant prose is breathtaking.

Our daughter, Julia, who smiled, encouraged us, and demonstrated infinite patience with long hours and late dinners. Our brother, Don Hughes, and all of our parents, families, teachers, mentors, clients, and adversaries, and the grace and pluck that have gotten us each this far along the crazy paths we call our lives.

Julio and Terrie would like to acknowledge the Newfield community of graduates, learners, and colleagues for enchanting us with their presence and enriching us with their thinking, passion, and thirst for learning. We are want to thank the Newfield team for their many gifts, but especially for the mood of joy and service they bring to work every day.

G. Lee Salmon would like to thank his senior coach colleagues for sharing their client case studies and the senior managers at NASA, EPA, the Intelligence Community, and the Department of Treasury for their generosity and willingness to share material from coaching interventions in their organizations.

# *Introduction*

**W**hat is the connection between coaching and emotional intelligence? How important is that connection, and how powerful? Why would you want to help your clients improve their ability to consciously apply what are basically subjective communication skills?

There is only one reason why you would want to help your clients develop their emotional intelligence, but it is a very good one. Emotion is the power that connects human beings to everything they care about! Without emotion we cannot tell what is valuable, or why it is, or how much time and effort we should spend trying to get it or get away from it! Throughout this book we will present compelling evidence that emotion is what makes our lives exciting and meaningful and worth the enormous amount of effort it takes to enjoy authentic success.

We wrote this book on the process of coaching your clients so you can help them further develop their emotional intelligence. We developed and organized this specific material to help that group of dedicated men and women called coaches make their best contributions to transforming the social, economic, and spiritual evolution of human civilization. This is not a grandiose description of their work, but is in fact what effective coaches do, and if we look honestly and unflinchingly at the world today we will see that this transformation is the superordinate task that must be accomplished, and it cannot be left to them alone. Mere survival is no longer an option for our species and cannot happen if its thrival does not occur! This means that in order for our species to be able to survive it will actually have to reach the level of synergy and integration at which it is thriving! That makes this transformation everyone's primary task: the coaches', the clients', senior leadership's, the shareholders', and the customers'

Coaching is an example of the critical cultural development process Alfred Korzypski called time binding. The father of general semantics realized that what made humans' evolutionary success possible was their ability to use language to transmit the evolving vision and understanding of civilizations accomplishments from one generation to another so that the amount of time spent in reinventing the wheel was minimized. There is *no* time left for that today! Coaches must be able to effectively communicate the way to develop the enduring relationships of authentic success.

The need for the coaching profession exists because somewhere in the dark days of human history fear and superstition confused us. We misunderstood what was happening and built some false premises into our reasoning as if they were true. As we continued to build our history on this flawed understanding, we grew more and more distracted and the balance between advancing our collective needs and our individual desires tilted increasingly toward the individual.

We misinterpreted the meaning of our growing material success and the comforts we enjoyed became a kind of decoy that misled us. The problem and its solution both lie squarely with the authors and readers of this book and the clients who will seek us out to learn how to make more effective emotional connections with the people, causes, and things they care about. As it is today, huge numbers of the most affluent and best educated people in the United States (and elsewhere) are conditioned to spend their time desperately pursuing a false, inauthentic version of "success." It has become a collective habit, and perhaps the most destructive aspect of this syndrome is that when we *do* seem for a moment to achieve the fleeting goals it offers, our very success nurtures further craving. This becomes the kind of profound insatiability that only an addict understands, "You can never get enough of what you don't really need." When we attempt to meet our subjective emotional needs through the acquisition of objects, the virus we now call consumerism spreads. It becomes more and more like a cultural cancer that increasingly requires objectifying the very people with whom we are in relationships.

Our focus in this book is to present an antidote, a prescription for treating this kind of spiritual dislocation. We believe you will be very happy to discover a number of elegant solutions with which you can help facilitate the development (in yourself and your clients) of the authentic emotional skills that will address these challenges. When you are successful at helping them learn how to engage their emotional energy and better communicate the emotional meanings of their lives they will be very grateful to you—and so will their colleagues at work and their spouses and children at home!

In the 1966 version of *Alfie* when Ruby asks of him, "What's it all about, Alfie?" she is demanding to know why she should be expected to faithfully contribute to their relationship at the expense of her desire for commitment, when, instead of living by "that old golden rule" he is constantly seeking relationships with other women behind her back. Alfie hasn't a clue what it's all about, but if he wanted to learn and hired you for his coach and you had read this book, you could definitely help him discover his own answer, and it would *assuredly* include developing his emotional intelligence! But Alfie isn't the only clueless client out there. Jenny in *Forrest Gump* and Professor Higgins in *My Fair Lady* would all live much happier lives if they could be your clients and get you to coach them on improving their use of emotionally skillful means.

When Thomas Hobbes described the life of man as "poor, nasty, brutish, and short," he was observing the erosion of emotional intelligence that ensues when everyone comes to perceive that they are in competition with everyone else. (In his case it was within a pre-industrial economy.) Cognitively it seems that concern about the quality of our relationships is a luxury we cannot so easily afford when the pressures of hunger and poverty and sickness are constants in our lives. When we are able to sink into the more central awareness of subjectively organized reality, we can easily see that this is when it counts the most!

Now machines have relieved a vast percentage of the drudgery from our lives and almost everyone in the developed world enjoys a material opulence beyond our ancestors' wildest dreams, yet affluence leaves us feeling uncertain, inadequate, hounded by the constant pressure of time, and the sense of competition of each with every other has only increased.

There is a very delicate balance that our species must master in order to avoid its own self-destruction. We must clearly perceive and commit the correct amount of time and energy to achieving our individual well-being and correctly allocate the amount that must go to securing it for our families and communities. Spending too little on either side of the equation will cause the systems within systems to perturb and, if they go too far, to fall apart. Developing emotional intelligence is our insurance against these sorts of calamities because the process requires learning how to value ourselves *and* value others as well as cultivating an awareness and sensitivity for when this dynamic is getting out of balance.

What must be done when we notice that one side or the other is starting to run low? It takes real courage then to discipline our own desires and delay their gratification so we can attend properly to the needs of others. On the other hand, when we have grown accustomed to the appreciation and mutuality that come from attending to others and our relationships with them, it takes an equal but different kind of courage to pull back into the more solitary work of satisfying the personal and spiritual needs that are unique to our specific souls. It is only through learning to accomplish all of these that we can ever enjoy the authentic success of a human life fulfilled.

Until recently much of the human research project was devoted to discovering how our environment and the external "things" in it worked. We would then apply this knowledge on behalf of improving our life conditions by, for instance, making our ships sail faster with a new type of mast, or developing a vaccine for a previously untreatable disease, or engineering a heat-resistant coating that would enable us to cook without our food sticking to our cookware. Millions of improvements in hundreds of domains made our lives easier, longer, and considerably more comfortable.

But beyond a certain point, the abundance of new and better things could not serve our deeper needs. It gradually became apparent that the real work of human beings had much more to do with improving our ability to collaborate and work together than with facilitating the burn rate of our consumption. Now a radical shift in our capacities is required if we are to integrate our economic and social efforts in such a way that they deliver wisdom from our knowledge, justice from our abundance, and real freedom from the myriad of our opportunities.

This is the revolution we find ourselves in the midst of today. Whether it has been officially named yet or not, this is the Relationship Revolution and all the professional coaches who are helping individuals and teams increase their emotional effectiveness are central to what is fueling its success! The relationship revolution is not only transforming our relationships with the things and processes and people that are external to us in the world, but the most radical transformation that it propagates is in our relationships with our selves! It is only as we begin to discover our relationship with the whole field of being that constitutes and includes us as individuals that we can truly bridge the gaps and transcend the differences that now lure us into violently destructive competition instead of realizing and stewarding the self-renewing abundance that is this planet's nature.

In order to solve the vast number of problems that our disorientation has caused, we must learn to work together effectively, understanding that our *real* motivations are all shared, discovering how to prevent conflict and how to resolve it elegantly when we cannot, learning how to help each other access the optimism and commitment necessary to succeed in the largest challenge our species has ever faced.

Within all of this complexity there also lies simplicity, for no matter what these challenges look like on the surface, at the core they are issues of emotional management. How we manage our influence on the single field of emotional energy that fills the workplace, the family, and all of our communities will determine the amount of flow and the amount of resistance we encounter in this work. It will determine the amount of time we spend or waste and whether or not we accomplish this sacred goal.

# Emotional Intelligence as a Foundation for Effective Coaching

In the first part of *A Coach's Guide to Emotional Intelligence* we establish how the competencies of emotional intelligence and the principles for applying them balance to form an excellent foundation for a sound coaching methodology. The second chapter specifically makes the business case for developing emotional intelligence through the coaching process.

We invite you to consider approaching the processes that we outline in this book as a developmental journey. The book will serve as a map that familiarizes you with the field of relationships coaches need to be proficient in if they want to succeed at the goal of helping their clients develop emotional intelligence. We expect that by the time you finish the book you will have a clear understanding of what emotional intelligence and emotional and social effectiveness are, why they are important, and specific steps to take in helping your clients begin their own developmental journeys.

A critical part of reaching any destination is being able to define it in such a way that you will know when you have arrived. We employ a highly successful technique known as "outcome specification," which was developed in the early work of neuro-linguistic programming (NLP). This method requires that you help your clients define what will be different in what they will see, what they will hear, and how they will feel when they have accomplished the changes they are seeking. This exercise actually provides their subconscious minds highly specific targets that, once set, they will then continuously pursue.

The business case for the interface of coaching and emotional intelligence reveals that executive coaching is a growth industry across the globe. In the UK, executive coaching has been described as one of the fastest-growing professions. Boyatzis (2006) described executive coaching as one of the few rapid growth industries in the last few years in the United States. In part this is because of the vast number of problems that coaching as a solution set effectively addresses. In Chapter Two we cite some of his work on EI practices that have demonstrated measurable success.

Researchers studying the impact of executive coaching reported that when managers, coaches, and coachees were surveyed and asked to select which topics they were most interested in developing, all three groups selected four common items as the most important: Developing Self, Self-Awareness/Self-Reflection, Career Advancement, and Building Relationships. Three of the four are direct emotional and social effectiveness (ESE) skills.

The numerous examples of research in this chapter drawn from literature strongly support the case that there is a direct relationship between the level of emotional intelligence competencies within an organization and their bottom-line profitability.

# CHAPTER 1

# Connecting Emotional Intelligence and Coaching

There is an urgent need to develop emotional intelligence in our organizations, teams, and families. For decades the contributors to this book have diligently studied and responded to the challenges of developing of a more emotionally and socially intelligent work, and we have done our best to synthesize the most valuable aspects of our discoveries here. It may be helpful to imagine the encounter we are about to share as a journey and this book as a guide that maps out the field of relationships you will need to understand in order to succeed at the goal of helping your clients develop their emotional effectiveness. We will do our best to familiarize you with the territory and the road signs, as well as help you develop the skills for negotiating this journey, both on your own behalf and for the clients whom you serve.

First, we will describe the destination we are seeking to reach and how we will know when we get there. Second, we will talk a little bit about who is welcome on this journey and who we are likely to be meeting along the way, and third, we will define some of the ideas and concepts that serve as signposts along the way.

# THE DESTINATION

As we said, this book is about one thing— helping you help your clients become more emotionally effective throughout all aspects of their lives. This means that by the time you finish your journey through this book and we have explored the territory of *coaching for emotional intelligence*, you will have a clear understanding of what emotional intelligence or, as we prefer to call it, emotional and social effectiveness is, why it's important, and what specific steps you can take in working with your clients to help them begin their own journey of exploration and development, or if they have already begun, to accelerate it, or guide the journey into destinations that are even more interesting and satisfying to them.

The fact is human beings don't change unless they feel discomfort or the hope of greater comfort and satisfaction somewhere else. Your clients will engage in the transformational process of developing their emotional and social effectiveness (ESE) only if they believe it will help them accomplish those two sorts of changes. How will you know if you're making any progress? Because both kinds of change involve a certain amount of stress, as your clients become more authentically successful, their faces and bodies are likely to look more relaxed, particularly around their eyes, shoulders, waists, and hands. They may walk more gracefully, and they will probably speak in voices that sound calmer, more confident, more relaxed, less tightly wound. The tonal range in their voices will increase, you will hear lower and higher tones, and their voices will likely sound less dry, less brittle. In their bodies they may report feeling softer, freer, with a wider range of motion, moving more slowly, gently, and certainly being more relaxed. Emotionally you can expect them to feel happier, more optimistic, and most likely better about who they are and the level of influence they are able to exert over their worlds.

But these are only the general kinds of landmarks that you will be able to detect as a result of your clients reaching their coaching destination. If you want the measures of your clients and your success to be even more specific, then you will need to ask them what the concrete, physiological indicators will be that most persuasively demonstrate an increase in their emotional and social effectiveness.

This strategy for outcome specification was developed in the early work of neuro- linguistic programming. It is a highly successful technique that calls for asking your clients to describe what will be different using the three primary sensory channels that organize social interaction. What will they see, what will they hear, and how will they feel differently when they have accomplished the changes they are seeking to achieve. As a result of having this discussion they will give their subconscious minds concrete targets and routes that they can then follow continuously day and night until the goals have been accomplished and their realities are remodeled. Moreover, it gives you and your client specific measurable points for charting your success. Of course, it's normal for clients to shift their goals as they gain deeper understanding of what they really want. When that happens, be sure to update your map of success.

## YOUR TRAVELING COMPANIONS

Coaches of all levels of accomplishment from the highly experienced and seasoned practitioners to the brand-new coaches who are just beginning their training—all are invited to join this expedition. Some of you may serve your clients as life coaches, helping them work through the personal issues in their lives, while others may coach in one of the many domains of business and leadership coaching. You may coach teams of engineers or teams of hockey players; the skills you will be learning here are equally relevant to all these groups of clients because it is their emotional energy and their ability to manage it that helps them achieve what they value in their lives.

## SIGNS ALONG THE WAY

Now if you will, allow us to familiarize you with some of the terminology that will serve as signposts for our exploration. Doubtless we should define what we mean by coaching and emotional intelligence. Both of these terms have many definitions, and we certainly do not claim that ours are the right ones, but they are specific enough to help you make the best use of the instruction that follows.

**Coaching** facilitates a specific kind of teaching and learning relationship in which the coach has a higher degree of experience and expertise in certain areas that the client wants to develop for him or herself. In order for it to be effective, the relationship cannot be a one-way street, both coach and client need to encounter each other openly and honestly, willing to accommodate and incorporate the changes that their relationship will entail. The responsibility for initiating the change lies most squarely in the client's court, while maintaining the momentum is a responsibility that each party must fulfill. The relationship can take place in person, over the telephone, or both, and it is never sexual in nature. There are specific International Coach Federation ethical guidelines posted at www.coachfederation.org/ICF/For+Current+Members/Ethical+Guidelines/. All coaches should familiarize themselves with these principles and consider sharing them with their clients.

**Emotional Intelligence** (EI or EQ) is the name of a field of inquiry that explores how human beings apply their subjective, non-cognitive behavioral skills to successfully manage and improve their relationships and life conditions. It is a term of art that is broadly recognized throughout the academic and professional communities. EI distinguishes between learned behavior and the inherited characteristics which are measured in part by IQ assessments.

**Emotional and Social Intelligence** directly includes the realm of social wisdom and engagement. It has been a part of much of the EI research from the beginning, such as that by Reuven Bar-On, creator of the BarOn EQ-i®. Boyatzis and Goleman have added it to their measure, which is now the Emotional and Social Competence Inventory (ESCI). Because the focus of coaching centers on your clients' engagement with themselves and the world, we believe that the "social" part of this concept is indispensable to effective coaching.

**Emotional and Social Effectiveness** (ESE) is the term we primarily emphasize in this book and in our work. We find that in practice the term "intelligence" is often intimidating. On the other hand, the term "effectiveness" implies can-do possibilities. We can authentically emphasize effectiveness because, unlike the elements of IQ, the elements of ESE are based on competencies that can be learned and enhanced.

While emotional intelligence (EI), emotional quotient (EQ), emotional and social intelligence (ESI), and emotional and social effectiveness (ESE) are intended to be interchangeable for purposes of this book, we will primarily focus our discussion on ESE and the generic name for the field, emotional intelligence or EI.

**Clients** is the term we use to refer to the people being coached. You might also use other terms, such as coachee or co-workers if you are an internal coach.

**Observer-self** is a term used to refer to the practice of metaphorically stepping back and neutrally observing your active engaged self. It heightens awareness and supports more intentional choices.

**Life Conditions** refers to the opportunities, resources, and limitations that make up the field of engagement in which living creatures conduct their lives. A snail and a horse and a human all have life conditions, and they are drastically different, however a well educated white man working in America and an equally well educated African-American woman working in the same company can also have radically different life conditions that have nothing to do with the qualifications we mentioned. The man could be a single parent of a child with disabilities, while the woman could be single, and unaware that she just picked the winning lotto numbers.

**Ontology** is a philosophical term referring to how we think about being and existence. Because emotional intelligence is measuring subjective capabilities that profoundly influence how successfully we exist in the world, the ontological viewpoint provides a powerful complement. Because emotional intelligence contributes so much to how we understand who we are in the world, how we communicate those aspects of our nature, and how we engage those aspects of others, it can be considered an ontological concern. We want to familiarize you with the notion of ontology along with our other definitions because it is an important landmark we will visit in the material about Ontological Coaching™ presented by Newfield Network later in this book.

Here is the simplest "official" definition we could compile (thanks greatly to Wikipedia). Ontology is a point of view from which philosophy considers questions like: "What things really 'exist' and what is their nature?" It studies how we conceptualize reality and the nature of being. To support this with a tiny bit of context, there are four categories of questions that philosophy asks: "How should one live?" (ethics), "What counts as real knowledge?" (epistemology), "What are the principles of correct reasoning?" (logic), and "What things really 'exist' and what is their nature?" (metaphysics). Ontology is a central branch of this last category, which investigates being and what types of things can be said to exist in the world, and how they are related.

Most significantly perhaps, ontological investigation helps us distinguish our being from our doing, who and what we are from what it is we do. In a world that places entirely too much emphasis on the latter, assuming an ontological vantage point can liberate us and restore balance to our perspective. (See Observer-self above.)

**Somatics** is the field of study that considers the degree of bodily awareness that is active in a persons life and the amount of influence it contributes to their authentic success. Balance, proprioception, and spontaneous right action are some of the topics it may address.

## COACHING TO BUILD EMOTIONAL AND SOCIAL EFFECTIVENESS

Coaching for emotional and social effectiveness is a process of helping others learn how to express and receive emotional energy in ways that strengthens their connection with others and builds more effective relationships. This requires that both people be able to recognize and accurately decode the meaning of the emotional energy patterns in the conversation. It includes helping your clients learn effective strategies for managing their own emotional energy and that of the others around them. While the communication can be done through intimidation or obsequiousness, there are far more forthright, elegant, and effective ways that can be learned through helping your clients increase their emotional effectiveness.

In our relationships with other human beings, we exchange emotional energy and information that lets the other person know two very important things: (1) how socially receptive we are. Are we interested in engaging with another in conversation and interaction, or do we want to be quiet or even left alone? and (2) how motivated we feel. Do we feel a driving need to accomplish some goal, or are we peaceful and content? Relating to another individual requires attention, energy, and a willingness to regulate our behavior, respectively, in ways that facilitate meaningful exchange, for instance, holding up our end of the conversation without being dominating.

In order to be open and sensitive enough to recognize and understand what others are feeling emotionally, we need to have a certain amount of curiosity and trust in ourselves and the environment. We have to be able to encounter others and relate to them with minimal defensiveness. We also need to hold as a fundamental position that our relationships with others are intrinsically valuable, rather than existing only for what we can get from them to benefit ourselves.

Another excellent practice is to assume that everyone (including our clients and ourselves!) always makes the best decisions available at the time. Humans are not wired to be able to choose against their immediately perceived best interests, even though ideally they could have or "should" have made different evaluations and taken different actions. This helps us keep our own judgments from further impeding our clients' progress in the change process.

## CONNECTING THE FIVE ESE PRACTICES AND EI MEASURES

Coaches assist clients in myriad challenges that are usually complicated by a variety of life conditions. It could be learning to manage up with a difficult boss, influencing an unmotivated employee, or deciding on a career shift or whether to get married or divorced. Given the breadth of potential coaching relationships, we highlight five central emotional and social effectiveness practices that will help you address the EI development challenges you encounter in your coaching work. These are bigger-picture concepts than the specific behavioral skills measured by EI assessments. In coaching you're called upon to assist your client in effectively applying clusters of these skills, and based on our experience and research, we believe the clusters most central to coaching for ESE are: Valuing Self, Valuing Others, Responsive Awareness, Courage, and Authentic Success. These practices take the concepts measured by the three primary emotional intelligence measures and pull them together into the five practical outcomes you and most coaches are likely to focus on with your clients.

Reuven Bar-On, creator of one of the most popular EI measurements, wrote "The Bar-On Model of Emotional-Social Intelligence (ESI)," an articled published on the EI Consortium website at www.eiconsortium.org/research/baron_model_of_emotional_social_intelligence.pdf. This article presents a useful overview of his instrument and in it he describes the three major EI models thus:

> The *Encyclopedia of Applied Psychology* (Spielberger, 2004) recently suggested that there are currently three major conceptual models: (a) the Salovey-Mayer model (Mayer & Salovey, 1997), which defines this construct as the ability to perceive, understand, manage and use emotions to facilitate thinking, measured by an ability-based measure (Mayer et al., 2002); (b) the Goleman model (1998), which views this construct as a wide array of competencies and skills that drive managerial performance, measured by multi-rater assessment (Boyatzis et al., 2001); and (c) the Bar-On model (1997b, 2000), which describes a cross-section of interrelated emotional and social competencies, skills, and facilitators that impact intelligent behavior, measured by self-report (1997a, 1997b) within a potentially expandable multi-modal approach including interview and multi-rater assessment. (Bar-On & Handley, 2003a, 2003b)

The topic of measurement is extraordinarily relevant to the field of emotional intelligence, because until EI could be measured accurately and proven to exist, it was discussed (and often dismissed) as soft skills, people skills, warm fuzzies, group hugs, and the like. These three reliable and scientifically valid assessment instruments changed all that. Those three are the BarOn Emotional Quotient Inventory, the MSCEIT developed by John Meyer, Peter Salovey, and David Caruso, and the ESCI developed by Richard Boyatzis and Daniel Goleman. And there are other instruments that have also contributed to development in this field.

The research to develop and evaluate these instruments demonstrated that emotional intelligence is a feature of being human that can be measured. Next it became a matter of demonstrating, particularly to the business community, that improving the emotional intelligence of leaders and followers within an organization could be measured as real dollar savings to the bottom line. Over the past ten years this has also been increasingly well documented by such organizations as Multi-Health Systems, which publishes the BarOn EQi and the MSCEIT assessments and regular articles on the topic of R.O.E.—Return On Emotion. You will learn more about the business case in the next chapter.

Many coaches find it vital to use EI instruments as a part of their coaching practice; and we respect that many coaches work without using instruments. That's your choice. If you do work with one of the major three, the following chart provides an overview connecting the scales of the three EI instruments with the five ESE practices Each practice is shown with the constituent competencies from each of these models. These choices are based on our many years of experience. If you work with any one of these measures, you might list the skills differently. That's fine. This is presented as a guideline for working with any of the three primary measures and understanding how they influence development and application of the five ESE strategies. Our recommendation to you is to read our chapters on them, consider our suggestions, and then add in your own experience, training, and awareness of your clients. This will help you focus on the specific skills each client most needs in order to develop competency in the practice you are working on.

The five practices and related skills from the three EI instruments are:

| EQ-i | MSCEIT | ESCI |
| --- | --- | --- |
| **Valuing Self** | | |
| Self-regard | | |
| Emotional self-awareness | Perceiving | Emotional self-awareness |
| Empathy | Understanding | Accurate self-assessment |
| Flexibility | | Self-confidence |
| Happiness | | Emotional self-control |
| Optimism | | Adaptability |
| | | Optimism |
| **Valuing Others** | | |
| Emotional self-awareness | Perceiving | Emotional self-awareness |
| Empathy | Understanding | Emotional self-control |

*(Continued)*

| EQ-i | MSCEIT | ESCI |
|------|--------|------|
| Interpersonal relations | Facilitating | Transparency |
| Flexibility | Managing | Adaptability |
| Optimism | | Empathy |
| Social responsibility | | Teamwork/collaboration |
| Reality testing | | Optimism |

**Responsive Awareness**

| EQ-i | MSCEIT | ESCI |
|------|--------|------|
| Emotional self-awareness | Perceiving | Emotional self-awareness |
| Assertiveness | | Accurate self-assessment |
| Empathy | Understanding | Emotional self-control |
| Flexibility | | Adaptability |
| Impulse control | | Empathy |
| Stress tolerance | | Teamwork and collaboration |
| Reality testing | | |
| Social responsibility | | |

**Courage**

| EQ-i | MSCEIT | ESCI |
|------|--------|------|
| Self-regard | | |
| Emotional self-awareness | Perceiving | Emotional self-awareness |
| Self-actualization | Understanding | Emotional self-control |
| | | Self-confidence |
| Stress tolerance | Facilitating | Adaptability |
| | | Initiative |
| Assertiveness | Managing | Empathy |
| | | Organizational awareness |

| EQ-i | MSCEIT | ESCI |
| --- | --- | --- |
| Independence | | Teamwork and collaboration |
| Reality testing | | Change catalyst |
| Impulse control | | Optimism |
| Optimism | | |

**Authentic Success**

| EQ-i | MSCEIT | ESCI |
| --- | --- | --- |
| Self-regard | Perceiving | Emotional self-awareness |
| Emotional self-awareness | Understanding | Accurate self-assessment |
| Assertiveness | Facilitating | Self-confidence |
| Independence | Managing | Emotional self-control |
| Self-actualization | | Transparency |
| Empathy | | Adaptability |
| Social responsibility | | Initiative |
| Interpersonal relationships | | Optimism |
| Stress tolerance | | Empathy |
| Impulse control | | Organizational awareness |
| Reality testing | | Service orientation |
| Flexibility | | Developing others |
| Problem solving | | Inspirational leadership |
| Optimism | | Change catalyst |
| Happiness | | Influence |
| | | Conflict management |
| | | Teamwork/collaboration |

You might notice that Authentic Success includes all the skills identified for each measure. It's the most comprehensive practice of the five and draws on all of your client's potential.

## TEAMS AND GROUPS

We have just discussed working with individuals and expanding their EI. But what about teams? For purposes of measuring a team's EI we have developed the Team Emotional and Social Intelligence Survey™ (TESI®), which is a team 360. Teams evaluate their performance and capabilities in the seven core skills of identity, motivation, emotional awareness, communication, stress tolerance, conflict resolution, and positive mood. Using the term "360" indicates that it's a circular perspective on the team. If you work with groups, you can cross-map the five ESE practices with those seven skills as the key challenges demand and discover the specific areas of challenge for your work group and how to resolve them most elegantly.

We have also found working with the EQ-i Group Report effective. This report is an amalgamation of the individual scores of the members of the group or team. It includes the benefit that each member receives an individual report, something we believe to be quite helpful whether you are using this report, the TESI, or other measures.

## COACHING FOR ESE CALLS FOR MULTIPLE PERSPECTIVES

In order to reach our three audiences eager to learn how coaches can help their clients apply the best practices for developing emotional and social effectiveness, the five of us have merged our efforts and extensive experience from our various areas of expertise. Writing for Collaborative Growth, James Terrell and Marcia Hughes have addressed how specific emotional intelligence competencies can be developed through the coaching relationship. Writing for Newfield Network, Julio Olalla and Terrie Lupberger have introduced the powerful role that emotional learning plays in ontological coaching. Writing from twenty years of experience as a leader in the federal government and a New Ventures West trained coach, Lee Salmon discusses the transformational effects that coaching to develop emotional intelligence has produced for leaders in several key U.S. government agencies. Each of us has common and unique values that influence the world we see, the way we describe it, the passion that inspires us, and the self that emerges from our unifying commitment to contribute content that will prove valid and useful to our readers.

Among the many recognitions we gained from collaborating on this project, one stood out above all the rest. The interface of coaching and the field of emotional and social intelligence is vast and can be imagined and approached and presented from a wide variety of perspectives. Our intention here is not to present a uniform philosophy or methodology; rather it is intended to facilitate new learning that will stimulate your thoughts, memories, and curiosity about emotional and social effectiveness in ways that invigorate your coaching practice with new insight and elegant interventions.

In *A Coach's Guide to Emotional Intelligence* we seek to illuminate the relationships between coaching and learning and emotional development from new angles and diverse reference points. As we mentioned, whether you are a seasoned and well-established coach, someone just starting in the profession, or somewhere in between, you are welcomed as the coaches and consultants and trainers who will best be able to take this learning out into the world and use it most powerfully on behalf of your clients and organizations. We look forward to many other books and articles on the topic of coaching others to develop emotional effectiveness, because we recognize that our effort has only scratched the surface. So please accept our invitation to explore and explain your own experience of how developing emotional intelligence in your clients has benefited them and the teams and organizations they work in.

There has never been a time that calls as loudly for all of us to help "reveal the hidden splendor" of our emotional connectedness and facilitate its effective engagement in the workplace, our communities, the halls of education and of government, as well as within our families and our personal lives. For it may well be our ability to respond to this invisible domain of energy and successfully fulfill that responsibility that will finally reorient us, bridge our perceived differences and reconnect us with each other, our collective purpose, and our miraculous planet.

# CHAPTER 2

# The Business Case for Building Emotional and Social Effectiveness in Coaching

## Marcia Hughes and James Terrell and Guest Author G. Lee Salmon*

*In hard times, the soft stuff often goes away. But emotional intelligence, it turns out, isn't so soft. If emotional obliviousness jeopardizes your ability to perform, fend off aggressors, or be compassionate in a crisis, no amount of attention to the bottom line will protect your career. Emotional intelligence isn't a luxury you can dispense with in tough times. It's a basic tool that, deployed with finesse, is the key to professional success.*

HARVARD BUSINESS REVIEW (2003, P. 5)

---

* To the extent the views expressed in this article are those of the author, G. Lee Salmon, they do not reflect the official policy or view of the Bureau of Public Debt, the Treasury Franchise Fund, or the U.S. Department of Treasury.

This chapter gives you material from which you can answer the question: "What's in it for my client?" Imagine you suggest to your clients that their coaching plan be designed to develop their emotional and social effectiveness (ESE) and their first response is "Why?" There is a real connection between financial success and developing emotional intelligence to base your answer on. We will explore that in this chapter and discuss the benefits that will interest them. Coaching is a growth industry, and research has found that key areas clients and organizations most need addressed are based squarely on using EI skills. We'll review positive results from organizations such as American Express Financial Services. One of the most obvious needs for EI is in building and conducting effective relationships, so we'll draw the business case connection to EI and coaching in relationships between supervisors and employees and between organizations and employees. Finally, we'll visit the increasingly broad application of EI in the domain of the U.S. federal government. This chapter points you to the possibilities of tailoring your own business case for your client base.

Executive Coaching is a growth industry. Geetu Bharwaney, an executive coach specializing in EI competency development, reported that "coaching has been described as one of the fastest growing professions in the UK, involving more professionals than doctors and dentists" (2007). Boyatzis (2006) described executive coaching as one of the few rapid growth industries in the last few years. He notes the small amount of empirical research existing at this time on effective coaching practices and draws on one data set, described later in this chapter, on EI practices that demonstrated measurable success.

One study on the impact of executive coaching found that "more leaders now routinely deal with significant ambiguity, disruptive changes and pressures to perform in an increasingly global and diverse context. They are asked to be both strategic decision makers and masters of the soft skills required to effectively manage people" (Schlosser, Steinbrenner, Kumata, & Hunt, 2006, p. 8). The authors report that when managers, coaches, and coachees working in Wachovia, Credit Suisse, and Deloitte were surveyed and asked to select the topics from a list of forty-six capabilities and behaviors that they were most seeking to develop all three groups selected four items in common as important (p. 17):

1. Developing Self
2. Self-Awareness/Self-Reflection
3. Career Advancement
4. Building Relationships

Three of the four are direct emotional and social effectiveness skills. Career Advancement is built on the application of emotional and social effectiveness from the application of all five ESE strategies as well as technical capabilities. The final skill chosen, Building Relationships, is inseparably connected to emotional intelligence and the five ESE strategies. Valuing yourself builds your capacity to value others. The better you are at being aware of what is actually happening and to responding well, the more true your relationships will be, you use courage at times to refine the relationship, and all of this comes together in authentic success—relationships that demonstrate trust and loyalty.

Cherniss and Goleman (2001, p. 4) aptly state, "Look deeply at almost any factor that influences organizational effectiveness, and you will find that emotional intelligence plays a role." To coach executives effectively, understanding organizational needs is essential and most if not every component of organizational operations is affected by emotional and social intelligence. This includes hiring practices, employee motivation, satisfaction, retention, productivity, team performance, and customer relationships. When you work successfully as a coach with the five ESE strategies, you will have available a control panel that reveals your client's current emotional competency blend. Then you can use this information in partnership with your client as together you gauge and adjust the levels of essential skills needed to meet the organizational and life demands your client is facing.

The data that shows emotional and social effectiveness is fundamental to the bottom line of organizational profits grows continuously. In an inspirational display of emotional and social intelligence in action, leaders in emotional intelligence research have created the Consortium for Research on Emotional Intelligence in Organizations, generally known as the EI Consortium. This organization is committed to promoting the development and knowledge of EI research. Their list of business case examples for emotional intelligence can be found on their website, www.eiconsortium.org. The organization also has a book series known as Advances in Emotional

Intelligence: Research and Practice; Cary Cherniss of Rutgers University, Richard Boyatzis of Case Western Reserve University, and Maurice Elias of Rutgers University are the editors. The second book in that series, *Linking Emotional Intelligence and Performance at Work* (Druskat, Sala, & Mount, 2006), is an outstanding resource filled with chapters on current research with numerous EI applications for coaching. We'll cite a few of those examples here and encourage you to peruse the book to increase your awareness of the research on success in building ESE. Understanding the well-documented benefits of developing skills such as emotional self-awareness, self-regard, empathy, optimism, and self-actualization, all core EI competencies that support the five emotional and social effectiveness strategies, will help you focus your own coaching practice to maximize the benefits of ESE and to effectively present the business case for your services.

## SUCCESS THROUGH EMOTIONAL AND SOCIAL EFFECTIVENESS

American Express Financial Services was able to expand gross dealer sales from 18 percent to 46 percent based on EI investment with four cohorts of professionals. In an article by Luskin, Aberman, and DeLorenzo (2005) found on the EI Consortium website, it is reported that a year-long program designed to measure the effect of emotional competence and forgiveness training on sales and quality of life resulted in significantly positive results. "The overall average improvement in productivity was 25 percent, which compared to a corresponding 10 percent increase in sales for the market group reference samples. In addition, the stress levels of the thirty-six participants who completed the yearlong training decreased 29 percent over the year of the project, while their reported positive emotional states increased 24 percent. Quality of life, anger, and physical vitality measures also demonstrated statistically significant positive change" (p. 1). The program included training, using individual capability measures such as the EQ-I, and coaching.

Doug Lennick, who formerly served as a senior advisor to Ken Chenault, CEO of American Express, discussed the evolution and savings experienced at American Express Financial Service Advisors in his chapter "Emotional Competence Development and the Bottom Line" (2007). One component of his advice is to emphasize development, not just training. This is what coaching is all about. Training is important to build awareness of the concepts; the next valuable step is to add coaching to promote the regular practice it takes to develop sustainable behavior change.

A highly respected leadership development organization, the Center for Creative Leadership (CCL), compared the relationship between EQ-i scores and the results from their well-respected 360-degree leadership instrument known as Benchmarks®. CCL found ten of the sixteen Benchmarks factors were significantly related to the EQ-i subscales. The Center also studied why executives' careers derailed and found that a high percentage of careers are derailed for reasons related to emotional competencies, including inability to handle interpersonal relationships, difficulty building and leading a team, and difficulty changing or adapting. Developing these ESE competencies is often at the heart of the purpose of executive coaching (Ruderman, Hannum, Leslie, & Steed, 2001).

Richard Boyatzis is a leader in emotional intelligence research and a professor of organizational behavior at the Weatherhead School of Management at Case Western Reserve University where longitudinal studies were conducted that showed people can expand their skills in EI competencies during the initial learning phase and as time goes on. He describes the statistically significant improvement that occurred with four cadres of full-time MBA students who graduated in 1992, 1993, 1994, and 1995 (Boyatzis, 2001). Through the program they expanded their skills in all three of the EI clusters they measured—Self-Management, Social Awareness, and Social Skills. This is the type of data to use in building your answer when your client asks "What's in it for me?" These skills can be developed and make a sustainable difference.

To review a few other business case successes, many of which are found at the EI Consortium website noted above, consider these positive results:

- In jobs of medium complexity (sales clerks, mechanics), a top performer is twelve times more productive than those at the bottom and 85 percent more productive than an average performer. In the most complex jobs (insurance salespeople, account managers), a top performer is 127 percent more productive than an average performer (Hunter, Schmidt, & Judiesch, 1990). Competency research in over two hundred companies and organizations worldwide suggests that about one-third of this difference is due to technical skill and cognitive ability, while two-thirds is due to emotional competence (Goleman, 1998). (In top leadership positions, over four-fifths of the difference is due to emotional competence.)

- In a national insurance company, insurance sales agents who were weak in emotional competencies such as self-confidence, initiative, and empathy sold policies with an average premium of $54,000. Those who were very strong in at least five of eight key emotional competencies sold policies worth $114,000 (Hay/McBer Research and Innovation Group, 1997).
- Optimism is another emotional competence that leads to increased productivity. New salesmen at Met Life who scored high on a test of "learned optimism" sold 37 percent more life insurance in their first two years than pessimists (Seligman, 1990).

## IT'S ALL IN RELATIONSHIPS

Relationships at work are critically related to employee productivity and retention. Building the capacity to develop and maintain positive relationships is a core skill coaches and coachees address, and this is all about emotional and social effectiveness. One of the common reasons people leave a job is because of their relationships with their immediate supervisors. Marcus Buckingham and Curt Coffman (1999) of Gallup reported that three factors inspire motivation and productivity:

- The employee feels cared for by the supervisor.
- They received recognition or praise during the past seven days from someone in a leadership position.
- They believe their employer is concerned about their development.

The supervisors' capacities to demonstrate these behaviors are rooted in their ESE skills, as are the employees' capacities to positively engage with one another and their supervisors.

Buckingham and Coffman showed that employee engagement both in government and the private sectors is at a disturbingly low point (1999). The ability to recruit and retain "the best of the best" will require managers who can shift from traditionally being subject-matter experts to devoting a large percentage of their time in developing authentic, unique, and connected relationships with employees.

Tom Rath (2006) identified another relationship element that makes a radical difference in the quality of one's work experience—having a friend at work. Companies are beginning to recognize that friendships are good for business. Developing and maintaining friends requires emotional awareness and empathy, which tie together in the ESE strategy of valuing others.

## FEDERAL APPLICATIONS

The Office of Personnel Management (OPM) in the federal government has compared emotional intelligence competencies with its leadership competency model, which is based on five executive core qualifications—Leading Change, Leading People, Results Driven, Business Acumen, and Building Coalitions. A recent article by Gowing and others (2006) tracks the considerable overlap between the federal government competency model and the EI competency model evaluated by OPM. In 2006 OPM recognized the importance of emotional intelligence in effective leadership by adding a twenty-eighth competency—Developing Others.

At the third symposium held by the International Consortium for Coaching in Organizations in April 2007, in Washington, D.C., thirty-eight participants, including executive coaches and representatives from public and private sector organizations using coaching, dialogued about the future of coaching and its global impact. Recent policy statements from the Clerk of the Privy Counsel in the Canadian government and head of the U.S. Government Accountability Office pointed to leadership challenges in the 21st century that could offer an emerging role for leadership coaching. David Walker, Comptroller General of the United States, identified the need for development of ESE skills when he told the group:

"If we expect to successfully tackle issues like health care, immigration, education, energy, and the environment, we will need more leaders in the United States and around the world with several key attributes. These attributes are courage, integrity, creativity, and stewardship. By courage, I mean people who state the facts, speak the truth, and do the right thing, even though it isn't easy or popular. By integrity, I mean people who practice what they preach and lead by example. We need people who understand that the law and professional standards represent the floor of acceptable behavior. It's time all of us set our sights higher and do what's right. By creativity, I mean people who can think 'outside the box' and see new ways to address old problems while helping others to see the way forward. Finally, by stewardship, I mean people who leave things not just better off but better positioned for the future when they depart their jobs and this earth." (United States Government Accountability Office, 2006)

These sentiments were similarly voiced by The Clerk of the Privy Counsel, Kevin Lynch, the most senior non-political official in the Government of Canada, who said:

"As we make our way in the 21st century, we need to acknowledge that now, more than ever, Canada's public servants are being asked to do ever more complex jobs, in an increasingly complex global economy. What does this mean? For senior public servants it requires a strategic focus on where to engage. Rather than trying to be all things to all people, we must concentrate on doing a few things and doing them well. Our goal must be an agile and flexible public service. But most importantly it is about leadership. Leadership is not about working longer hours, or harder or taking on more responsibility, it is about engaging employees and clients, setting the agenda, taking risks and being a role model." (Karlin, 2007)

These two senior government leaders point to the challenges facing civil servants who must become more emotionally intelligent, develop ESE skills on their own or with the help of a coach, and demonstrate an ability to create employee engagement in new and profound ways that will give meaning to the concept of stewardship.

## WHAT THE COACH NEEDS

Boyatzis (2006, p. 82) offered insight into effective coach behavior through research on "people acting like coaches in a difficult arena, that of counseling people with alcoholism and substance abuse problems." There are few empirical studies thus far on the coach competencies related to positive behavioral change in clients he stated, so for this study he used longitudinal results from the Navy to identify success differentiators.

Boyatzis established the measure of effectiveness in working with this group of addicts as "the work performance of their clients following treatment. A work performance measure can be considered conservative (i.e., more difficult in which to show change) and a more difficult treatment goal than abstinence because it requires changes in the client's behavior, ways of dealing with others, and drinking behavior" (pp. 83–84). The final results of his detailed analysis are that empathy and emotional self-awareness distinguish effective counseling and, by association, effective coaching. This confirms what we know intuitively, the coach's empathy or sensitivity for his or her client is critical to success. Similarly, a coach must be aware of his or her own emotions before being able to work with the client to build or enhance this capacity accurately. As Boyatzis states "The coach has the responsibility to be able to identify and manage his or her feelings and reactions. Whether the coach uses this information as part of understanding the client or as a vehicle for suspending his own needs and anxieties, managing oneself is difficult if not impossible without a high degree of self-monitoring, or emotional self-awareness" (p. 93).

The results strongly suggest that counselor/coach competencies are central to effectiveness. The normal success rate for alcoholism counselors is about the same in the Navy as in the external world—67 percent to 70.5 percent, respectively, Boyatzis reported, yet the superior counselors in the study who had developed their ESE skills of empathy and emotional self-awareness more fully had a success rate of 87.2 percent. This is a marked difference! Use it as a part of your own business case for success. The coaching relationship is a two-way street and you need to bring your own EI into the relationship to achieve the desired results. Our guest writers from Newfield Network discuss developing these skills in Chapter Nine.

## LEARNING BY EXAMPLE

Throughout the book you will find coaching examples to demonstrate application of the skills we are discussing. Additionally, Chapter Eleven includes two case studies. The first involves an executive and the board in a family business challenged with habitual and negative relationship patterns. The other focuses on a mid-level leader and her challenges with her team as well as her considerations around whether she wanted to be promoted at that time in her life.

The three case studies addressed in Chapter Ten on federal applications show a number of examples where coaching has helped develop the five ESE applications. Coaching in the federal government will continue to focus on developing relationships between leaders and followers because without motivated and committed followers, there are no true leaders. This speaks to the importance of employee engagement and building relationships that are based on the foundation of ESE strategies.

With increasing attention on challenges such as the price of oil in the Middle East, genocide, and global warming, our need for leaders who can build results supporting global sustainability could not be more important. The ability of our government and business leaders to develop relationships and engage in meaningful global dialogue is critical, yet many of these leaders lack the ESE competencies necessary to build enduring relationships. We encourage you to continue developing your business case for success through making emotional and social effectiveness a vital part of your coaching—the world needs you and your clients to succeed!

In summary, you will advocate more effectively for the proven value of EI when you are certain that there is a strong business case supporting your EI focus with your client. You can draw on the success stories presented in this chapter and on how thoroughly EI development is being built into large systems such as within the U.S. federal government. Also, take responsibility for your own EI skills. Studies such as the one by Boyatzis show you will achieve greater results when you develop your own skills, such as in emotional self-awareness. Your own business practice will be enhanced by your solid skills.

# TWO

# Building Emotional and Social Effectiveness Strategies in Your Client

The five chapters in Part Two are designed to provide you, the reader, with understanding and guidance in how to develop emotional and social effectiveness as you coach your clients, be they individuals or organizations. We have focused on five critical areas for building emotional and social effectiveness

- Valuing Self
- Valuing Others
- Responsive Awareness
- Courage
- Authentic Success

When you assist your clients in effectively developing any of these vital competencies, you are on the path of assisting them with sustainable and transformative change. These five strategies affect one another, creating a tapestry of skills if done well. The connections among these five competencies are deep. For example, how can we truly value others if we don't value ourselves? It can't be done. However, if we overvalue ourselves and miss the beauty of what everyone else has to offer, we're on a narcissistic path that can't be sustainable and isn't emotionally and socially effective or rewarding.

No one needs to be perfect in any of these five competencies. Perfection is a mirage that gets in the way of risking and enjoying life. Thus your strategic engagement as a coach is essential. We recommend that you and your clients seek to understand their strengths and weaknesses in these five areas, then jointly select the area(s) of focus. Remember that our greatest point of power is with our strengths, so don't automatically focus on that which appears to be the weakest. You may choose to work with an emotional intelligence assessment instrument to support your understanding. We briefly discuss some of the most used instruments in Chapter One, and they include the Team Emotional and Social Intelligence Survey (TESI®) if you are working with teams or, for individuals, the EQ-i®, after EQ 360®, and after MSCEIT® or the ECI. You can gain more detailed information on most of these measures in our book, *Emotional Intelligence in Action* (2005). Whichever area you decide to focus on is likely to expand your client's capabilities in other areas because of the synergistic influence each capability exudes around the circle of emotional and social well-being.

Chapter Three, Valuing Self, emphasizes building self-confidence and self-worth. As these expand, you will be able to work with your client in taking self-worth to the greater outcome of expanding self-actualization. You'll find that this is the path to developing authentic success, which is Chapter Seven's focus.

Chapter Four, Valuing Others, taps into the work of being human, which requires that we willingly help each other solve the problems that limit our safety and comfort and the meaning in our lives. Fortunately, we are wired to be social beings. We value many aspects of others—their material possessions, their education, their spirituality. Some of what we value will be intrinsically valuable and support our ability to work together and collaborate even in the hardest of circumstances. Other forms of valuing others may be sheer envy and just get in the way of authentic relationships and valuable action.

Chapter Five, Responsive Awareness, calls for a powerful integration— choosing responses based on well-developed awareness. Responsive awareness has several components for your clients to address: being aware of how they feel, understanding why they feel that way, understanding how others involved in the particular situation feel and why, and taking informed and aware action.

Chapter Six, Courage, clarifies that the emotional and social effectiveness known as courage allows us to act on what matters most in the presence of danger, difficulty, uncertainty, or pain, accepting that there will be consequences without necessarily knowing what those will be, and taking action anyway without being stopped by fear or being sidetracked from a chosen course of action. Being courageous means more than speaking with courage. Speaking is essential, yet there are more dimensions to acting with courage, including our somatic responses in times of challenge, our ability to act and to trust.

Chapter Seven, Authentic Success, calls for developing the emotional and social intelligence skill of self-actualization, which is built on the expansion of many underlying capacities, including valuing yourself and others, happiness, and optimism. It includes being able to embrace the light and the dark sides of your life and challenges our getting caught in the "perfection" trap.

The quotations found in Part Two are from Julio Olalla, *The Ritual Side of Coaching* (1998).

*Act with gentle irreverence.*
*There are no sacred cows in coaching.*

# CHAPTER 3

# Valuing Self

A central feature of the personal and professional development that coaches seek to facilitate in their clients is the ability to value one's self in positive, appropriate manner. If we do not feel genuinely worthy of what life has to offer, we will not pursue our best possibilities, or we will not do so in a manner that will actually produce the desired results. In this chapter we explore how self-confidence and self-worth contribute to your clients' success in the workplace, as well as powering the continuous growth of their individual self-actualization. Without these they cannot reach whatever goals they have designed to constitute their own unique success.

Valuing one's self appropriately turns out to be a process of continuous development and lifelong learning. What we know ourselves to be continues to evolve over the course of our lifetime, unless we succumb to the convenient belief (usually just after thirty) that we have learned all we need to know and the-self-that-I-am is now pretty much permanent. In that case we conclude that we have arrived at the point in life at which we are adults and we get to make the rules for those in our lives who are younger, or junior, or dependent on us. This conclusion is a developmental cul-de-sac from which few escape without a wake-up call in the form of a serious loss or other crisis.

It is often the case that the central part of our work as coaches is to help our clients develop the crucial emotional competencies around self-confidence, self-respect, and self-worth. We will explore self-confidence in terms of trusting ourselves, and self-worth in terms of how we balance our wants and needs with those of others, which includes holding ourselves accountable.

## SELF-CONFIDENCE

Heredity and our early experience of the world have a profound impact on our self-confidence and what and how we learn later in life. They influence not only the direction in which we head, but whether we recognize the opportunities along the way and whether we will move toward or away from those opportunities. As early as the seventh month in utero, we begin constructing our model of the world out of the ceaseless stream of sensations that we record in our central nervous system, musculature, and at the cellular level of our physiology. These fundamental memories of our experience are encoded with all our pleasant and unpleasant associations and help determine *what we can notice* and what we choose to pay attention to. This process shapes all our later expectations and attitudes toward life and learning. From very early on, these memories serve to guide our behavior in terms of which kinds of things or situations we explore and which we avoid. Our self-confidence is built around the dynamic interplay of curiosity and fear.

When toddlers have developed enough strength and coordination to begin exploring the world on their own, one of the first dangers they need to learn about is getting burned. Because their reflexes are still too slow to protect them, knowledgeable parents will sometimes quickly dip the child's hand in some mildly hot water or touch it quickly against a plate that is hot from the dishwasher while associating the warning "Hot!" with that sensation. That way the child learns of the hazard without risking the pain or injury they might experience if they were conducting their exploration of the world on their own.

Eventually, through repetition, children learn what sorts of things they should expect to be hot enough to hurt them, and their accurate expectations serve as their first line of protection. This kind of experiential learning becomes the basis for our self confidence, but unfortunately not all of our learning is based on such simple cause/effect relationships, and some of the things that people learn to expect result from associating misinterpretations of their experiences with the objective realities of the world.

Suppose a three-year-old who has taken numerous baths successfully stands up while playing in the tub one time and slips, hitting her head and inhaling some water before someone can rescue her. It would not be unintelligent for the child to conclude that tubs and water are dangerous—because under certain conditions they most obviously are. The amount of pain and fear she experiences will certainly shape the way the event is coded in her memory, and so will the way her caregivers respond, both at the time of the incident and in the future. It is possible to *learn* to be traumatized by water from the cues that others give us and to respond with an "inappropriate" level of fear and caution whenever water is present. It is also possible for our caretakers to teach us how to stand up carefully in the tub and be sure there is something to grab if you lose your balance.

This is an example of how we learn self-confidence or self-doubt from our experience of the world. When you are coaching clients who have learned hesitation rather than initiative, this is the domain in which you may need to structure new learning experiences to assist them in rediscovering and rebuilding their self-trustworthiness.

Frank is struggling with a serious case of self-doubt as a twenty-eight-year-old lead supervisor at a stamped metal parts manufacturing facility. He supervises three production lines on the night shift and has received an unsatisfactory performance review for failing to meet weekly production goals three times in the last six months. The first time it happened because a misshaped metal blank caught in the conveyor mechanism causing it to jam up and break. Finally, part of the conveyor got caught in the stamping area, which destroyed one of the dies. This resulted in the line being down for the next four shifts and the loss of productivity cost about $48,000.

If Frank had acted more rapidly, the damage to the conveyor could have been prevented and repairs could have been completed over the course of that night's shift so the line was up and running in time for work the next morning. The problem is that misshaped blanks, while infrequent, do occur once or twice a month and sometimes do make it through without any consequences beyond that piece being rejected as scrap—at a cost of less than $100.

The next two times there were problems with bad blanks, Frank over-reacted and hit the emergency shutoff, which put the equipment out of commission for around four hours while all the stamped blanks and those waiting to be stamped had to be manually cleared from the conveyor mechanism before it could be restarted in automatic mode. This cost over $5,000 and was hard on morale for several days because everyone knew they would miss their production targets for the whole week.

Frank's manager is confused and worried because he had high hopes for Frank and had seen him perform excellently for several months until the first incident. It has been recommended that Frank get some coaching from you to help him "settle down and get back in the game" because any more problems with production quotas will probably result in his termination. You are Frank's coach, and he has just given you the above explanation. You are aware of the substantial connection between how he holds his body and his ability to access his self-confidence. To get the energy flowing, you first help him understand how he's freezing his posture, and thus his creative thinking. The result is his self-confidence is dying from lack of breath.

*Frank:* So basically that's the story of why I'm here.

*Coach:* I understand. It sounds like you are seriously worried that one more mistake either way will cost you your job.

*Frank:* [nervously] That's right, and a month ago my wife had her hours cut, and we just learned our daughter needs oral surgery and braces.

*Coach:* It seems like you're under an awful lot of pressure *right now* [implying that this is only temporary]. How are you holding up?

*Frank:* Not as well as I'd like, I'm afraid. I just sit at my station and stare at the capacity monitors; I don't even go on break anymore.

*Coach:* How many monitors are there?

*Frank:* There are two for each line. One shows the average output for the last two hours, and the second shows the current rate of production.

*Coach:* Pretend you're at your post, and show me how you sit while you're watching the monitors.

*Frank:* Okay. [He sits up straight and stiff with his hands on his thighs and stares intently.]

*Coach:* So how do you feel right now, sitting that way?

*Frank:* Well, I feel tense.

*Coach:* What else? What do you feel in your hands and arms?

*Frank:* Tight and kind of shaky . . . it's actually pretty unpleasant, and this makes me wonder how I manage to sit like that all day long.

*Coach:* It looks congruent, like you're actually sitting there at the machine. I suspect this posture and this way of sitting are very familiar to you. What do you see?

*Frank:* I feel tired . . . and worried . . . anxious.

*Coach:* Good. Now tell me what you see.

*Frank:* I see the monitors, that and about five or six feet of wall space.

*Coach:* Great, Frank. Thanks for being willing to play along with me. Now stand up and shake it off. [Frank does, breathing a sigh of relief.] Now imagine you're home watching TV and sit in your chair like you're relaxing on the weekend. [Frank sits back down slouching and pretends to point an imaginary remote at the screen.] It's a whole different world, isn't it Frank?

*Frank:* [He nods, smiling for the first time.] If you say so [chuckling]. It's amazing how I'm sitting in the same chair but the feelings are totally different.

As Frank's coach, the next steps will be to help him find room to breathe and relax so he can access his skills and re-connect with his self-confidence.

## SELF-WORTH

Our self-worth reflects a pattern of evaluations we learned to make about how much of the time we should expect our efforts to be successful and/or accepted versus how often they will be unsuccessful and/or rejected. Over time we build this set of conclusions about what to approach and what to avoid into the comprehensive unconscious value themes that guide all our behavior. Remember, emotional energy is what connects us to every-thing we value. We learn to value being cautious or we learn to value being exploratory. We learn to value setting measurable goals and following a planned approach to achieving them or we learn to value a more sponta-neous strategy for discovering and satisfying the desires that motivate our behavior.

In the process of all this learning, we began to develop "our" point of view, a unique way of seeing the world through which we relate new experiences to our past learning, using it as a standard for evaluating and selecting our actions. Of course, there are many other factors that go into the development of our way of seeing the world (such as our intentions and moods and our explanations of why things are the way they are that may or may not be serving us). We have and will continue to discuss these throughout this book. The resulting preferences are not inconsequential; they end up shaping *what we can see* and how we behave in the world. For example, what sort of relationship do we tend to develop with quality and accountability? How do we assess the quality of our own work? How do we know when it is good enough? Does the approval of our efforts by others tell us when we have done enough? Is it when we *have* enough that we finally know we have *done* enough? Is it even possible for one to *ever* do enough . . . or have enough?

If our clients have not asked these kinds of questions of themselves, asking them as their coaches can help them learn to value themselves and their work more fully. These are the kinds of questions that strengthen self-accountability and lie at the heart of self-discipline and self-control. Other questions that can help us value ourselves more fully include asking: Is the value of our work determined by the amount of tasks we accomplish and how rapidly, or by the quality it expresses? Is our primary emphasis on quantity or quality? We generally learn to set these kinds of standards based on what has paid off for us in the past, but it is often uncomfortable life conditions that inspire us to create new visions!

Janice is a sales manager for a national health insurance company. She heads a team of seven salespeople, and their nickname in the department is "The Closers." They have seldom if ever missed reaching their quota and are deeply admired by the rest of the people in sales. But not everyone holds Janice and her team in such high regard. Customer Service refers to them as "The Headaches" because just about every week they get a call from some small business owner who is furious about how a feature of the plan they were sold does not apply in certain circumstances—specifically, their circumstances!

As the manager of customer service began to notice how much time, attention, and ultimately revenue these complaints were costing, she began to research the files of past cases and called some of the small business owners to try to clear things up. It turned out that Janice and her team were aggressively promoting every possible benefit of the company's insurance plans while minimizing the exclusions, or failing to mention them altogether. Bruce, the vice president of sales, was dismayed when this was brought to his attention and, in a lengthy meeting with her, placed Janice on a performance improvement plan the general thrust of which was that she must hold herself and her team accountable to a higher standard of responsibility to their customers.

Because of your experience in coaching some members of the senior management team, you have been selected to help Janice succeed at achieving these additional objectives. You are beginning to get acquainted with her in your first meeting when she asks:

*Janice:* How is that they happened to choose you to work with me?

*Coach:* I suspect it's because they're familiar with my work. I've done coaching with some members of the senior leadership team, and they were happy with the results. Because of that I also have some insight into the company's culture and values and some sense of how they hope to see them expressed.

*Janice:* I used to think I did too, and I really felt like my contributions to the bottom line demonstrated that.

*Coach:* I happen to know that your vice president has been consistently pleased with your team's contribution to the revenue of this organization. What he has become concerned about is the hidden costs that have been coming to light.

*Janice:* And what might those be?

*Coach:* Well, he must trust us to figure that out together, because he didn't tell me. [Even if he knows, the coach does not want to start off this relationship in the role of accuser.] What sorts of things did he mention to you?

*Janice:* Customer service is upset because there have been some complaints that we didn't cover the exclusions to coverage well enough when we sold some of the policies. Now in all of our sales presentations we will be required to mention them explicitly.

*Coach:* Hmmm. . . . [Pausing for a moment to let her words build resonance with her internally] Well it sounds like you have accepted this as a fact of life [reinforcing the truth of the matter], but it's not something you are too happy with? [Acknowledging her feelings and leaving room for her to correct that observation].

*Janice:* Look, I know this is a disciplinary action and there's no point in you trying to sugarcoat it.

*Coach:* Wow, it sounds like you feel I'm trying to sugarcoat this because. . .? [He leaves room for her to finish the "You feel _____, because _____." model we will describe in detail in Chapter Five.]

*Janice:* . . . because you're being all nice, and positive, and optimistic.

*Coach:* Well thank you. . . I guess, but I'm not trying to sugarcoat anything, Janice. If this is a disciplinary action, it's meant to be one in the original sense of the word discipline, because that was about the relationship between teaching and learning. But it's also possible to see this as punishment. Is that how it looks to you?

*Janice:* Of course it is!

*Coach:* Well, you still have your job. Have they said anything about taking away any of your past bonuses? [Still refusing to buy into her ploy of self-pity]

*Janice:* No, they don't have to. They can just humiliate me and my team in front of everyone.

*Coach:* My understanding is that they see you as a real asset to this organization, and they want you to be able to play at a higher level of responsibility.

*Janice:* [Just looks at him uncertainly—half suspicious, half hopeful.]

*Coach:* I suspect you're going to have to learn to manage more concerns at once and still produce a healthy share of the profit. It will take some effort, and it won't necessarily be easy at first, but the skills you need fall squarely within the realm of emotional intelligence, which just so happens to be my expertise.

*Janice:* What do you mean emotional intelligence?

*Coach:* That's what they call it in the world of HR and MBAs. Personally, I prefer to call it emotional effectiveness, because it's really about how effectively you communicate emotional energy and information through your behavior.

*Janice:* Okay, but what does that have to do with selling insurance?

*Coach:* I'm surprised you're asking me. That's your realm of expertise! How long a period does a new policyholder have before they renew?

*Janice:* It depends. Some policies renew after twelve months, some renew January 1, and others renew the beginning of the company's fiscal year.

*Coach:* So the longest period of time customers have to wait before they choose their insurance carrier again is twelve months?

*Janice:* [*hesitantly*] Yes, that's true.

*Coach:* One of the skills in the field of emotional effectiveness that I often help people improve is the skill of reality testing. This is the process of confirming with others that you are perceiving and understanding the objective facts of the situation accurately. In this case it takes significant investment for your organization to gain new customers; the reality checks are how satisfied they are and how long your organization keeps them. For your homework, I'd like you to get together with the customer service manager and figure out how many of your customers chose a different insurance carrier at the end of their first policy year in the past twelve months.

*Janice:* That's cruel!

*Coach:* Maybe . . . that depends on how you see yourself, and whether you believe the changes in your job description are a punishment or an educational opportunity.

*Janice:* If you think you can sell me that load of crap, you're crazy!

*Coach:* If that's what it was, I couldn't sell it, but I think you'll find it's a novel point of view that may be just what you've been looking for. You are motivated by measurable targets and concrete goals—am I right?

*Janice:* You set my team a quota, and we will reach it, or more likely exceed it—and that's why they call us "The Closers"!

*Coach:* Okay, 95 percent customer satisfaction after twenty-four months.

*Janice:* How in the world can you measure that?

*Coach:* Actually, there are probably many sophisticated and complex ways, but let's say if they renew their policies at the end of their second term you can assume they're satisfied. Part of your problem has been that you were not being measured in the most critical part of the process—the relationship. Companies have to have health insurance. They're going to buy it somewhere, your firm has a competitive product line, and you and your team know how to help people make a buying decision, so what's the problem?

*Janice:* If they're unhappy at the end of twelve months, we lose a customer and it will be pretty hard to sell them again. If they're still happy after twenty-four, we've still got the sale.

*Coach:* You've still got the *relationship* . . . and you and everyone on your team can sell more and earn more as soon as you learn how to deliver authentic care to your customers. When you look back on this, what do you think will have been the toughest part for you guys?

*Janice:* You make it sound like we've already done it. . . . Well, it'd be telling potential clients about all our weaknesses as well as our strengths.

*Coach:* Bruce still wants you to sell as much—and more—insurance as you were. He doesn't want your sales presentations to be all about what your policies won't cover. You can't be naïve or petulant. What will have been the toughest change you had to make?

*Janice:* [Silent a long time] If I pretend we've got some new formula that already works and try to reverse engineer it, what was hardest to accomplish was figuring out the right balance of what the customer needs to know. What will force them to buy versus what will ensure they choose us with eyes wide open and don't complain about being misled when something isn't covered?

*Coach:* Bingo! Now why is that going to be so hard?

*Janice:* It's going to take forever! We're going to have to figure out all these possible scenarios; it will take forever!

*Coach:* You're close, keep going. . . .

*Janice:* It will take more time to prepare. It will take more time to present.

*Coach:* So, what will you have to do?

*Janice:* We'll just have to speed up and cover more topics more quickly. But . . . but . . . Oh no! [Everything in her demeanor shifts] This means we're going to have to *slow down!*

*Coach:* [Silent at first] Interesting, maybe so—[he is slowing everything down right now!] but from where I sit, it seems that, by slowing down, you will spend more time and pay more attention to what each customer wants specifically, and the organization may get more repeat sales. It won't be nearly as tough or as painful as you imagine once you and you team members begin increasing your empathy skills.

*Janice:* This is going to make meeting with my team worse than meeting with my peer in Customer Service.

*Coach:* Janice, I do my best not to give advice, but for what it's worth, this will probably be some. When you go to meet with your peer, be very direct in your apology, but not subservient. Tell her *you* made some mistakes that *her* team had to pay for, and that you're sorry, and that you intend to make sure it doesn't happen again. She will probably feel pleased to have your acknowledgment and relieved that maybe she won't have to deal with so many irate customers. I doubt that she's going to jeopardize all that by gloating.

*Janice:* Okay, I'll give it a shot, but what am I ever going to say to my team?

*Coach:* Think about that for your homework. We'll discuss a possible strategy next time.

## HOW WE DEVELOP OUR SENSE OF SELF-WORTH

Developing our sense of self-worth is also a process that begins very early in life. For several days or even weeks, the life of a newborn is exclusively one of meeting critical biological needs. Gradually over time, as his or her memory of pleasant and unpleasant experiences begins to expand and stabilize, desires to repeat those that are pleasurable and avoid those that are uncomfortable begin to emerge. For the most part, however, newborns want only what they need.

Later in life our desires increasingly diverge from our needs as the sense of individual identity asserts itself. By age two a strong sense of preference is well-established through the body's identification with the "wanter" and "chooser." This set of drives plus the associated memories of success and failure in meeting them becomes the personality that captains the ship for a very long time—and sometimes forever. At least for the next twenty years, we are clearly off to the races while the nervous system grows and stabilizes and a capacity for self-reflective conscious thought gradually matures. As a part of this process, the personality not only learns how much of the time it can expect to be successful in meeting its needs and satisfying its desires, but it also learns some kind of balance between altruistic behavior and that which is self-serving.

In other words we learn how and when to manage our desires (and even our needs sometimes) so that our individual behavior will serve both our self-interest and the collective efforts of our society to thrive. In spite of our advertising-driven media culture's promotion of the attitude "It's all about me!" most people learn an acceptable balance between attending to their own needs and desires on the one hand and those of their community on the other. During times of rapid change and uncertainty when the social order is more chaotic, the more evolved members of the community will take up a greater share of the slack by increasing their contribution (for instance, grandparents raising their grandchildren). Similarly, those charged with enforcing the social will (the police) will do so more rigorously.

## SELF-WORTH TO SELF-ACTUALIZATION

The idea of authentic self-worth clarifies the difference between service and self-importance. The delicate balance between these polarities must be balanced in a way that promotes the individual's ongoing development toward self-actualization while simultaneously increasing social integration. Being able to enjoy the satisfaction of achieving the goals that we set for ourselves increases our feelings of self-worth, optimism, and happiness, as long as these gains are never made at the expense of others.

Coaching others in developing their self-worth can be an exercise in helping them extend the range of their accountability and social responsibility as much as it is one of helping them to increase their assertiveness and independence. However, there will certainly be times when you will encounter clients who need to recognize and develop new options for action because they have been consistently challenged by attitudes and behavior patterns that were learned from living in pervasive conditions of significantly limited resources.

If you recognize that someone's feelings of self-worth are limited by these kinds of deficits, your work as coach is to help your client begin discovering new resources, or discovering new strategies for developing new resources, or maybe simply discovering the possibility that new resources can be developed! In such situations, giving extra attention to demonstrating your humble respect for the miracle that they are and all that they have accomplished will help avoid the chances of coming across as judgmental. Working on self-worth is generally not something people can succeed at in an atmosphere of public critique.

## COACHING FOR EMOTIONAL INTELLIGENCE—VALUING SELF

Suppose you are called to assist a manager who works in the federal bureaucracy and will be retiring in five years. She wants to advance one more level in the system to achieve the maximum possible pay grade, but she doesn't have a college degree and the next level will require supervising many more people than she has in the past. In your first session she spoke about having to "fake it" a lot to get by in her career, but you can see that she is actually very competent and likely to succeed at the next level of responsibility. She needs to discover and connect with this level of competency in herself so that her feelings of self-worth will support her congruently in supervising the larger teams of employees.

She opens the session like this:

*Sharon:* I've thought about what you said, but I am pretty sure that they will all see right through me and realize I've just been faking it and lucky all these years.

*Coach:* I'm not sure how you could accomplish such a hoax for so long if that's really what it was.

*Sharon:* Well, all I ever really did was *get to know everybody I work with and make friends.* [Translated: all she did was build a reliable network for effective emotional communications.] Then when I needed things somebody else did, we'd just ask each other and help each other out. That would never work on such a large team.

*Coach:* Why not?

*Sharon:* Well. . . . I just don't know. There are too many things happening that need to be done.

*Coach:* Yes, you're absolutely right. You would be supervising more projects, but how does the work get done on the project you're responsible for now?

*Sharon:* That's the whole point—the other people do it, I don't!

*Coach:* Sharon, what you are describing is exactly the way the best leaders and managers help their employees be successful in the workplace. They care about them in a way that earns their respect. They ask them to help out on the projects where they can contribute best. They watch their work just enough to notice whether problems are starting to show up, and when they notice that, or even suspect it, they ask for an update on the progress of the project.

*Sharon:* But I've never been to college except for a few classes I took at night. Everybody who would be reporting to me will have a degree. How will I know enough for them to respect me?

*Coach:* Respect has a whole lot more to do with qualities like openness, honesty, direct communication, how much people can trust you, how consistent you are, and a lot less to do with how much knowledge you have. It's also grounded in your technical skills at accomplishing your mission. How long have you worked in this agency?

*Sharon:* It will be eighteen years next month.

*Coach:* How many people have been here longer than that?

*Sharon:* Well, there's a couple, maybe three.

*Coach:* During that period of time I imagine you've seen the mission of this agency when it was being accomplished at its best and at its worst.

*Sharon:* Yes, you're absolutely right about that, and we are finally starting to hit our stride again!

*Coach:* Then who could be better for this job than you? You know the people and they know you. The senior leadership team trusts you. Can you tell what the agency has to do to succeed over the next few years?

*Sharon:* Yes, no question about it, we have to consistently apply the same set of metrics we developed during the last administration, no matter what kinds of political changes occur.

*Coach:* Who can make the best business case for doing so in your area of the operation?

*Sharon:* [pausing] I can . . . I guess.

*Coach:* I know that, and I think everybody around here knows that and they are hoping and expecting you will apply soon. Who would you need to talk to here in order to feel convinced about whether or not this is a good decision?

*Sharon:* I have to talk to my manager and the man who holds the position now and maybe one or two people on his team.

*Coach:* Are you willing to do that before we get together next time?

*Sharon:* Yes, I guess I am.

*Coach:* Well, I don't see anything else I need to cover here. There is little bit of time left in the session. Maybe you could spend it scheduling some of those meetings now. And, in our next conversation let's investigate whether there are any new skills or knowledge that will help you do a really great job in this next position.

*Sharon:* Okay, I'm beginning to think this might actually be possible . . . and maybe even more fun.

You can see how the coach's ability to generate new learning simultaneously affords the client an opportunity to discover new potential in herself and new options for action. Even small successes gained in a direction that has traditionally been difficult for us are tremendously reinforcing and can help us outgrow the excuses and limiting explanations that previously curtailed our emotional effectiveness and depreciated our sense of self-regard.

In this chapter we explored how self-confidence and self-worth contribute to your clients' success in the workplace, as well as powering the continuous growth of their individual self-actualization. We saw the critical role that these ingredients play in reaching the goals that constitute their own unique success.

*Without trust there is no relationship and without relationship there is no coaching.*

# CHAPTER 4

# Valuing Others

Helping your clients learn to authentically value others (and communicate that they do!) is a crucial responsibility in the coaching relationship. In this chapter we will explore why it is critical for the coach to be able to teach his or her client how to value others in a way that is both compelling and authentic. We will also cover why it is so important and powerful to do this. We list the four reasons why society grants public value to its members and the critical roles respect and trust play when our clients seek to reflect the value that they experience in their relationships with others.

The work of being human requires that we willingly help each other solve the problems that limit our safety and comfort and the meaning in our lives. The work of organizations isn't much different, and fortunately these are the kinds of relationships we are wired to develop and we have done precisely that over thousands of generations since our species began, perhaps as cave dwellers on the African savanna. You may be surprised to consider how even mundane things we take for granted require far more relationships and joint efforts than at first we may imagine.

An excellent example is simply driving to the store to buy a carton of milk. Where do we start in our process of recognizing and appreciating the efforts of all those who make such a purchase possible? Do we start with the dairy farmer who was out milking his herd yesterday at 5:30 in the morning? Or the corn farmer who a year earlier planted and harvested the corn the cows ate for food? Or do we go back to the assembly-line workers who assembled the tractor that the farmer used to plow the fields and plant the corn?

Every step of the way the people involved utilized their relationships with each other to make the work go more smoothly and accomplish tasks in which they themselves were not as highly skilled. How often were those relationships collaborative? How often were they conflictual? Obviously, we can't know, but we can surmise that when people respected each other, shared pertinent information openly and honestly, and held themselves and the other people accountable to an agreed-on standard of quality, they were far more successful. That is the payoff of collaboration. When the people were not respectful or trustworthy or working in agreement around shared expectations and promises, the relationships were no doubt conflictual and most likely unsuccessful.

## EVERYONE WANTS TO CONTRIBUTE

Being authentically successful in the world is much easier when you understand one thing: No matter what someone's age or gender or nationality, no matter what his or her health or wealth or sexual preference, no matter how introverted or extroverted or strong or weak or good-looking the person is, everyone wants the opportunity to contribute to the process of life in a meaningful way that receives the acknowledgment and approval of the others in the social group. Everyone naturally wants to be noticed and accepted and cared about. Everyone who doesn't understand that, or doesn't do that, or doesn't know *how* to do that, is going to be far less successful than if he or she did! Enter the emotional intelligence coach.

Fortunately, it is possible to help people learn how to better perform the behaviors that communicate caring. Unfortunately, for some people who are particularly task and outcome focused, that is all they want to learn— how to *perform* the behaviors necessary to secure cooperation from others. Fortunately, our limbic brain can spot a fake a block away, and unless participating in the charade meets some need of ours; our subconscious mind will disqualify the communication and mark as untrustworthy the person who delivers it.

So then is it possible for a coach to help his or her clients improve their capacity to authentically care for others? Absolutely! If your clients genuinely want to discover the immense contribution that valuing others can bring to their own lives and their workplace relationships, they certainly can do so, and a skillful coach in emotional effectiveness can surely help them.

One of the first things our clients will notice when they begin giving a higher quality of attention to the people around them is that this kind of social connection is a two-way street. The respect and care that they begin to extend will begin to return to them as others come to trust that their interest is sincere. It is probably just human nature that if someone who has typically been rather distant suddenly begins to be more friendly and inclusive one day, we wonder, "What does *he* want?," but over time as your client's positive concern proves genuine and consistent, suspicions fade and the warmth and trust of human camaraderie is extended in return . . . obviously according to each individual's personal level of comfort and capacity.

Perhaps through assessments or interviews or even just the grapevine, you might learn that valuing others is not a skill your clients excel in yet. Suppose they congruently challenge you to show them what kind of return can be expected on their investment of time and effort in developing emotional effectiveness? How do you help your clients appreciate what may always have lain outside their field of attention?

Remember: Everyone wants the opportunity to contribute to the process of life in a meaningful way that receives the acknowledgment and approval of the others in their social group. The exceptions to this rule of thumb start to show up in some people who think they're smart enough, or rough enough, or rich enough to make, take, or buy whatever they want without depending on the good graces of others. And there's some truth to this. If you're important enough, or powerful enough, people *will* do what you want—either in the hope of gaining your favor or avoiding your wrath. Still, it remains a fact that kings need subjects to rule over, and pop stars are dependent on their fans to be a phenomenon. Human beings just don't fare well in isolation, and down deep everybody knows and honors that, no matter how self-important and exclusive their behavior may seem.

As a coach there will be times you need to bring this to your clients' attention in ways that don't directly antagonize or alarm them. Really believing that one is special and somehow more important than someone else is a huge blind spot and a liability that time and fate are generally certain to disabuse one of. Coaching work teaches people how to integrate with the team or community that wants to support them in the accomplishment of mutual visions, dreams, or promises.

## HELPING PEOPLE VALUE OTHERS

Helping your clients value others often requires helping them value themselves more authentically. We have all known people who felt the need to increase their social status or sense of self-worth by diminishing others.

Seasoned coaches understand that their clients have learned from living where to set their expectations, and that until or unless *they* set about changing them, that is where they will remain. As a coach it is important to understand consciously that there are least four different kinds of worthiness that our society (by collective agreement) grants its members and publicly recognizes: physical, educational, economic, and spiritual worth.

Humans have always granted status based on physical attributes like strength and speed and beauty, because for the very longest part of our history, the problems we needed to solve in order to thrive and keep civilization marching forward were physical. As our technology and symbolic information processing skills began to increase at an ever-increasing speed, so-called "knowledge work" became the most highly valued and most highly paid type of work in the developed world.

A cartoon from the early 1980s captured society's struggle to integrate this fact in a conversation between two Roman galley slaves. They sit side-by-side chained to the giant oar of a huge ship and under the suspicious eye of a mean-looking guy with a whip. One says to the other, "I'll have you know, the only difference between me and Caesar is that he has access to more information!" Ah yes, vive le difference!

In some circles of society we value others because of their educational status. This could either be because of the degrees they have achieved, and the associated assessment that this means they are intelligent, or for how well they communicate their knowledge of the world and how it works. Often these people are able to apply their education to the kinds of problem solving that are highly rewarded in the economic sector. However, those whom we value most highly for their education and intelligence are the individuals who are able to gracefully blend their cognitive, emotional, and social intelligence to communicate with us in ways that help us think more clearly, feel more alive, and act more effectively. Who knows—this might even be a coach!

What constitutes credible markers of worthiness in the economic sphere is very well known due to the way in which consumerist values are constantly promoted by the media. How much we own, who we know, what our title is, how much compensation we command, the quality of our clothes and toys and furnishings, how big our homes are—in this realm this is what determines status and significance. If your clients have a hard time valuing people who are more or less economically successful than they are, that is a ripe territory for coaching which can ultimately lead to the client's increased sense of self-value and compassion.

Transactional coaching strategies could be employed in this situation to help them build their skills, hold themselves to a higher level of accountability, and increase their confidence in their performance. Transformational coaching strategies could be employed to help them discover new perspectives from which to understand their relationships with work, other people, and success. In both cases, helping the clients to explore and recognize what they want in order to be satisfied and getting them into actions consistent with that recognition ultimately will lead to a greater sense of self-worth and also increased valuing of others whom they perceive to have more than they do. We explore the differences between these two approaches in coaching in much more detail in Chapter Eight.

The last sphere of influence we are going to discuss in which communities grant their members a sense of social worth is the spiritual domain. The theistic ethics of Judeo-Christian cultures recognize all human beings as having an equal intrinsic worth by virtue of being children of the same creator. Even though this does not cut much ice in the marketplace, it is an important presupposition that most members of society will agree to, and you can use it to help clients who consistently see increased profits and saving time as more valuable than interpersonal relationships. More developed individuals recognize that it is actually these relationships that form the foundations that provide all the real support for the bottom line.

We have already discussed the importance of valuing yourself in the previous chapter, and now we want to emphasize how significantly it contributes to the capacity for valuing others. As much as Western culture may worship the notion and achievements of the individual, we often overlook the fact that we cannot live or work effectively except in relationship to others. There is no "I" without a "you." We are social beings. With extremely few and rare exceptions, individuals go through life relating to others at many levels of engagement. This emotional capacity of valuing others is not just a nice "skill" to have, it is a critical practice which determines our effectiveness in day-to-day living. Valuing others isn't just a good idea or moral obligation, it is a vital necessity to coordinate our action effectively with others if we are to derive any real satisfaction and meaning from our lives.

Some of us accomplish the early learning that so deeply affects the way we see the world in situations in which reading the emotions of *others* accurately is critical for our success and safety. If there are people in our infancy and childhood whose emotional states fluctuate dramatically and capriciously between acceptance and rejection, learning to read their feelings and how to accommodate them will command the majority of our attention. We may well develop remarkable skills for discerning the subtlest cues about pending changes in their emotions from their nonverbal behavior, but this may often come at a cost to our own self-awareness and well-being. For these kinds of clients, learning to more fully value themselves becomes a central challenge to their development as adults and their ability to value others.

## LEARNING HOW TO NOTICE OTHERS WITH RESPECT

The interpretations we learned to make about reality define our general expectations of life and our day-to-day relationships, as well as determining if and when they are satisfied. At the other end of the spectrum, coaches must also consider clients who may have received the doting attention of caregivers that zealously sought to anticipate and satisfy their every need. That sort of training can constrict a person's attention exclusively to his or her own sphere of concern and make attending to the concerns of others feel foreign and require extra effort and it sometimes makes it tough for the person to muster the patience necessary to do so! In that case, learning to value others becomes that central maturational challenge in adulthood.

While there are obviously innumerable points of balance between these two extremes that produce different strengths and weaknesses in our emotional and social effectiveness profiles, new biological research is also identifying genetically determined set points for some of the neurotransmitters such as serotonin that significantly condition our emotional resources. In any case, negotiating the balance of nature and nurture and learning how to direct and focus and shift and sustain our attention is the work of a lifetime. It is the hard-won prize of developing the executive functions of the prefrontal cortex as well as our skills of emotional and social effectiveness.

## HELPING OTHERS VALUE OTHERS

*There is nothing more pleasant to a man*
*than the sound of his own name.*

DALE CARNEGIE

Dale Carnegie, who was a sort of a coach in his own right, identified some highly effective behaviors for communicating to others that we value them. Now, because one of his primary motivations was to coach men and women in becoming better salespeople, the question could certainly be posed, "But how sincere is that?" and we can authentically respond that in the first stages of helping clients develop and communicate their empathy, using a technique like calling the people you greet by name is sincere enough to engage an honest answer from them about their state of health or their attitude about the day. To begin, that is enough.

Maybe our client has never even looked up to greet the others in his or her office at all. The sincere appreciation of others grows in steps, sometimes baby steps. We must grant them the space to be only as sincere as they can be, and expect nothing more. Otherwise such a person will never open enough to savor the delight of a casual acquaintance sharing some simple story that touches his or her soul at the perfect time and confirms the common bond that holds, yet transcends, all personal concern.

Sometimes it takes the discipline of exercising a technique to help someone start seeing at an emotional focal depth from which they can finally begin to feel who other people are, what they care about, and why that matters. It takes energy to redirect our attention and begin distinguishing new features of reality that previously lay beyond our emotional perception. Learning someone's name and remembering to use it when you meet him or her is a pretty basic level of demonstrating respect, and because people do enjoy that kind of very specific attention, it works! It makes a stronger connection and opens the way to begin building trust.

## TRUST SHOWS VALUE

When we show people we value them, we open the way to strengthening and deepening their trust. When we demonstrate our own trust effectively, it will be easier for them to trust us and take more significant risks in return. However, trust calls for a deeper level of interpersonal commitment than simply valuing others requires. Trust includes placing our confidence in others and the willingness to risk some portion of our well-being on the basis of their character and promises.

A critical feature of trust that is sometimes overlooked is predictability. We are more likely to trust people when we feel we know what we can expect from them, when they look and act similarly to the way we do. Suppose your client is a videographer who is going to meet with a bride-to-be and her mother. Obviously, they hope to hire someone who can do an excellent job recording her eagerly awaited wedding. Your client will probably be more successful if you encourage him or her to show up in attire appropriate to the women's social class rather than in full biker regalia. An extended hand with a pleasant greeting of "Hello, my name is so and so" will probably be more successful in engaging their business than a surly "Yo, what up?" (Unless of course she is a second-generation hip-hoppin', biker chick!)

This is actually pretty obvious, even to those whose emotional and social effectiveness may languish a bit. But why? The fact that we recognize the inappropriateness of this costume mismatch so easily is an interesting "skill" in itself. It is something that we learn to do unconsciously through our primate instincts and a talent that our individual brains develop called implicit learning. It is our limbic brain that communicates the potential wardrobe miscue up to our cognition. Because it looks for agreement and a matching between posture, facial expressions, tonality, and other nonverbal dynamics in its memory such a clash of costumes causes major chaos!

The neurological capacity known as limbic resonance employs an invisible sending/receiving system to synchronize mammalian behavior, enabling a herd of racing gazelles to turn together on a dime or a milling crowd of uncertain and disgruntled people to become an angry mob in moments. In *A General Theory of Love*, the authors state "Mammals developed a capacity we call limbic resonance—a symphony of mutual exchange and internal adaptation whereby two mammals become attuned to each other's inner states. . . Eye *contact*, [emphasis ours] although it occurs over a gap of yards, is not a metaphor. When we meet the gaze of another, two nervous systems achieve a palpable and intimate apposition" (Lewis, Amini, & Lannon, 2000, p. 63).

The results of groups of mammals tuning to each other's internal states need not be limited to herds in panic and mob mischief; limbic resonance can also be seen and felt in groups of people singing patriotic songs together or in religious congregations intoning hymns of praise. It can be the silent eye contact between a coach and client that transmits the message: "*I'm* not going to say this, *you'll* have to admit it to yourself!"

Making ourselves mutually available to the connecting power of limbic resonance may be the act of trust that best communicates our willingness to value others. Often it occurs in those special moments in which the present trumps all regret about the past and fear about the future with an immediate meaning all its own. This is the place where coaches connect with their clients and their clients connect with co-workers and family to give and receive the profound value that knowing others brings. It lies beyond what can be measured quantitatively, far beyond the bottom line, and yet at the heart of every authentically successful organization.

Interestingly enough, there is a formula for facilitating this state prescribed in the teachings of virtually all human cultures. The Buddhists say, "a state that is not pleasing or delightful to me, how could I inflict that upon another?" (Samyutta Nikaya v. 353); the Jews say, "What is hateful to you, do not to your fellow man. This is the law: all the rest is commentary" (Talmud, Shabbat 31a). The Muslims say, "None of you [truly] believes until he wishes for his brother what he wishes for himself" (Number 13 of Imam "Al-Nawawi's Forty Hadiths). The Christians say, "Do unto others as you would have them do unto you." The Hindus say, "This is the sum of duty: do not do to others what would cause pain if done to you" (Mahabharata 5:1517). In Confucianism it is written, "Tse-kung asked, 'Is there one word that can serve as a principle of conduct for life?' Confucius replied, 'It is the word 'shu'—reciprocity. Do not impose on others what you yourself do not desire'" (Doctrine of the Mean 13.3).

## COACHING FOR EMOTIONAL INTELLIGENCE— VALUING OTHERS

As a result of a merger, your client has been placed in a challenging position. In her old role she was in charge of inspection and quality control, leading a team of three people. She presents as a dynamic and highly confident "go-getter," but in her new role she will also have to manage two inspection supervisors and the nine inspectors who will also report to her. As part of a cultural integration and leadership development initiative, she has completed an emotional intelligence 360 assessment and one thing that everyone agreed on was that her skills in assertiveness and decisiveness were matched by her self-regard, but there wasn't much of the openness and caring that makes a team feel their leader is accessible to them. She has approached you for help in this, although you sense her interest in development is lukewarm. This is your second session.

*Coach:* It's good to see you again, Jackie. As I recall, for homework last time I asked you to reflect on one or two things that were going to be significantly different in your new position.

*Jackie:* Yes, and I did. As we discussed, I guess I'll probably have to improve my soft skills some if I'm going to be able to succeed in managing five times as many people as I did before. It's a pretty big change.

*Coach:* You're so right, it's a pretty big topic. Let's talk about change for just a moment. There are different kinds of change we are called on to accommodate in life—ordinary day-to-day change that everyone has to deal with all the time, fundamental change, when something shifts that we had always successfully relied upon in the past, and drastic change when the new situation won't necessarily even resemble the old one at all. From what you told me last time, this sounds a little drastic. Are you sure you want to tackle this? [Contrary to how this may sound, the coach is not being prescriptive or judgmental here. This is the kind of provocative invitation that was needed to engage Jackie's ESTJ [Myers-Briggs] personality type. She won't have any trouble letting the coach know if she disagrees with her or doesn't want to explore some particular line of investigation.]

*Jackie:* Let's put it this way: My retirement is vested here, even though it will be about eleven years before I can touch it, and I know the industry and like it. This merger is going to take us out of the shadows and put us in the top eight companies nationally. It's the only job I can do here, and I sure don't want to move.

*Coach:* I appreciate your reputation for being a straightshooter, Jackie, so I'm going to call 'em like I see 'em, and not waste any time pussyfooting around. I think you may be getting in over your head.

*Jackie:* Wait a minute; my scores weren't low in everything. I can handle this. Besides, I thought you were supposed to be encouraging me. Is this some kind of a "coaching strategy" you're using on me?

*Coach:* You could look at it that way I guess, but I'm not playing games. I would call it reality testing. I'm concerned that you will have a pretty small window to succeed in and that other people may already have their eyes on that position. My question is whether you will be able to build alliances quickly enough with twelve people in order to get the traction you're going to need right out of the box? [Up to this point the coach has been working to disrupt some of the certainty that is in the way of the client's new learning. This leader is from the school of "Don't take it personally, it's just business." Learning to genuinely value others is tough for them because their attention has always been on the quantity of results, not the quality of relationships. Jackie is going to have to decide there is a good reason to allocate some of her attention to that aspect of leadership.]

*Jackie:* [A little defensively] I don't know; all I can do is my best.

*Coach:* Okay, good. You trust yourself; that's important. How can you earn the trust of new people quickly enough for them to follow your lead without a lot of testing? [Here the coach signals she is backing off and makes a true statement that is also a compliment, but quickly turns it around to expose some new territory that is decidedly unfamiliar for the client.]

*Jackie:* I don't know—a group hug maybe?

*Coach:* Absolutely not! Orchestrating a group hug requires that every single member of the team trusts you implicitly and trusts each other at that same level, *and* that a ritual is called for to honor a significant passage in the evolution of the group's accomplishments or accountability! If your timing is wrong with a group hug, they'll eat you alive.

*Jackie:* Okay, look, I was just joking.

*Coach:* Oh good, I'm glad. What *will* you do to earn their trust?

*Jackie:* I don't know, I've never really managed this many people before. [She may be skating a little bit here, but she is still taking some real level of risk. For her, just saying "I don't know" takes courage.]

*Coach:* It's not really any different than what you do with one person at a time. What kind of people do you trust, and what did they do to earn it with you? ["Earn" is chosen very purposefully throughout to impress the fact that this trust is something of major value.]

*Jackie:* [Thinking a long time while the coach remains silent.] I trust people I can tell are after the same results that I am.

*Coach:* Do they also need to understand what results you are after in order for *you* to trust them?

*Jackie:* Not always, but it definitely helps when they do.

*Coach:* The devil is in the details when it comes to results. How do the people you trust figure out specifically what it is you're after so they can let you know whether they're on the same page?

*Jackie:* Well, they watch me, they listen to what I say, and they notice what I work the hardest at. They ask me!

*Coach:* Yes of course, all that makes sense, but what lets you know that they *really* understand what it will take to make the results a success for you?

*Jackie:* That's obvious, they tell me, they show me and make comments or ask questions.

*Coach:* [Dead silent]

*Jackie:* Well, that's right isn't it? Isn't that what they do?

*Coach:* It definitely sounds like it is, in your experience, so assuming that's right, how do you go about earning the trust of the new people on your team?

*Jackie:* [Silent for a while, thinking] I guess it makes sense. I'll figure out what kinds of results they want to accomplish.

*Coach:* And . . . .

*Jackie:* And I'll let them know mine.

*Coach:* I can see you're giving this a lot of thought. Is it something you've ever intentionally set out to do with people in the past?

*Jackie:* No, probably not so directly.

*Coach:* So then, what kinds of things will you say when you're spending time getting acquainted with each one of them? [Here the coach installs a critical step into the process by presuming that Jackie will "spend time getting acquainted"!]

*Jackie:* I'll probably just ask them what kind of results they care about most.

*Coach:* Are you a good poker player?

*Jackie:* That's an odd question. Why do you ask?

*Coach:* Are you?

*Jackie:* I hardly ever play cards, but I'm probably pretty good at not tipping my hand if that's what you mean.

*Coach:* Good, because you're going to need your best poker face when you hear all the results they care about that may seem unimportant to you. If you frown and say or imply, "That's stupid!" no one is going to trust you, let alone follow where they need to be led.

*Jackie:* C'mon, give me some credit I'm not going to say "That's stupid"!

*Coach:* No, not with your mouth, but if you sigh, or roll your eyes, or shake your head, it will be the same thing. What if someone says that a result that he really cares about is feeling included as a member of the team?

*Jackie:* [Shaking her head] But that's not the kind of results I mean.

*Coach:* I know. But you will be better off if you pretend that it is, and just say, "Okay, tell me more. Why is that important to you?"

*Jackie:* How come?

*Coach:* Because even if we know someone well, we can never be 100 percent certain what it is he or she cares about at any given moment, and it's a much better way to facilitate further communication to accept whatever it is someone offers us without judgment. Yes, there may very likely be a time in which we may need to confront them and request that they do a much better job of reality testing than we think they have done so far, but not until we know everything we can about what they want and why they want it.

*Jackie:* Okay, I see, it's like you're doing reconnaissance and gathering intelligence so you can figure out what makes them tick.

*Coach:* Well, sort of I guess . . . but that makes it seem as if you're going to use the information you gather *against* them. I would rather think of it as active listening and that my goal for the information I learn about them will be to use it on their behalf, to help them succeed.

*Jackie:* Yeah, you're not really very competitive are you?

*Coach:* No, actually I'm very competitive, but beating out other people isn't generally as challenging or satisfying as improving on my own past performance or helping a team generate a much higher degree of productivity than they have ever been able to achieve in the past.

*Jackie:* But I'm someone who is committed to excellence and achieving *my* personal best, and I'm not about to let anyone do better than me if I can possibly help it.

*Coach:* I understand, Jackie, but your organization has realized that individual contributors are seldom able to bring as much to the bottom line as a team of individuals who have learned how to collaborate in their work together and are constantly competing with their own best record of performance. It does feel a little bit foreign at first, but once you get the hang of it, I think you'll find it offers a very exciting and challenging way to work on continuously improving your personal best. Besides bonuses are now going to be determined in a large part based on how well the team does in achieving its goals.

*Jackie:* Yes, I know, so I guess I'd better learn how.

*Coach:* That's the spirit! This week your homework will be to begin listening to others more attentively than you ever have before in your life: colleagues at work, family members, the clerks in the grocery store. You have one mission: make your very best educated guess about what's going on for them. Fill in the blanks as accurately as you can in the sentence, "You feel_____, because_____." If you don't get it quite right, they'll tell you and help you fine-tune your guess. I want you to test yourself with this pattern a minimum of 5 times a day before our next meeting!

*Jackie:* You're acting all positive and psyched up because you want to encourage me.

*Coach:* Very good! But how do I feel?

*Jackie:* [silently struggling for a moment.] Enthusiastic?

*Coach:* Bingo!

In this chapter we explored why it is critical for the coach to be able to teach his or her client how to value others in a way that is both compelling and authentic. We also covered why it is so important and powerful to do this. We described how society grants its members public value in the physical, educational, economic, and spiritual domains, and discussed the critical roles respect and trust play when our clients seek to reflect the value that they experienced in their relationships with others.

*Too busy explaining life, we forget to listen to it.*
*Most of all, we forget to love life.*

# CHAPTER 5

# Responsive Awareness

Responsive awareness is a strategy that brings together two core skills—being fully, consciously, aware and then taking action based on that awareness. This ESE strategy calls for a powerful integration—choosing responses based on well-developed awareness. In a simple, logical way, this strategy requires taking emotionally informed action. Responsive awareness is an emotional and social effectiveness strategy that goes for the gold by peeling back layers of understanding and taking integrated action, often responding to a complex myriad of factors, as we'll explore in this chapter.

So how do you as a coach work with your clients to get to this deepened response level? While there is no magic wand; there are practices you can guide your client to use, many of which we'll discuss. Based on your understanding of the key components of this strategy, you can also develop your own practices.

In this chapter we identify the four components to responsive awareness. We discuss the three parts to emotional literacy and how coaching to develop this literacy builds responsive awareness. We discuss the process for increasing awareness, and thus your clients' ability to respond effectively when you, the coach, mirror your clients' emotions and help them connect those emotions with their cognitive explanations about the behaviors and challenges that they are seeking to address in coaching. From this comes the ability to use their emotional energy effectively. To act, your coachee needs motivation and that is enhanced by awareness, so we discuss these steps to action and provide many strategies for building emotional awareness through reflective engagement. We discuss building awareness of the emotions of others, which connects with the discussion in Chapter Four on valuing others. Effective responses require understanding not only of one's own emotions, but also how others feel. Finally, we'll demonstrate a sample coaching session in which the coach works on building responsive awareness.

Responsive awareness has several components for your clients on any given matter. You can discuss with them the importance of:

1. Tuning into their awareness of what their body and emotions are telling them about how they feel
2. Understanding why they feel that way
3. Understanding how others feel and why—especially when they are the people whose actions you need to influence
4. Taking informed and aware action.

Being aware of how you feel and why requires accurate emotional self-awareness. Understanding others' feelings and emotions is built on the emotional and social skills of empathy and developing and maintaining relationships with lasting depth. All three of these skills are built on your clients' comfort with emotions and their being open to new ideas. The fourth step, taking emotionally informed action, is built on the emotional and social skills of being compassionate, flexible, assertive, realistic, and courageous. Here clients need to exercise impulse control, stress tolerance, and be socially responsible. If teams are involved, teamwork and collaboration are required. We'll discuss coaching to build responsive awareness, using emotional literacy and responding effectively throughout this chapter, but motivation is a non-negotiable skill. Without that, change won't happen. As coaches we can help our clients find the reason and resources to expand their motivation, but if change is to happen, it has to come from within.

We respond to emotional data throughout our bodies. Emotional awareness and strategic execution occur within different structures of our brains and, depending on how skillfully we have been taught to use those different structures, we might be an expert with one domain and just get ourselves in trouble with the other.

Responsive awareness is a tool for integrating the different ways we have of being aware, of being emotionally and socially savvy. Effective responses to troublesome situations first require new learning and then developing new habits. Building this new awareness occurs in the part of the brain referred to as the prefrontal cortex. New learning is possible, but undoubtedly it requires work. Rock and Schwartz (2006) explain the transition process, that new learning engages the executive center of the brain, and why the process of learning can be uncomfortable. Creating change requires energy and practice. It's only by repeating the process of activating neuronal connections and making that energy contribution repeatedly that a habit is developed; the new skill is then a sustainable change.

## THE COLLABORATIVE GROWTH COACHING PROCESS FOR RESPONSIVE AWARENESS

Responsive awareness is an important capacity for coaches to encourage their clients to explore and develop throughout the coaching relationship. Understanding why this is so requires that we consider the fundamental purpose of coaching.

Since our species first emerged on the planet, human beings have enjoyed whatever degree of freedom and comfort we achieved because of our ability to succeed at two things: (1) our ability to adapt to changes we cannot control and (2) our ability to cause the kinds of change that we desire. These can only be accomplished by learning—that is, imagining new conditions in the physical world, attempting new behaviors to bring those conditions about, remembering which worked the best, and repeating and improving on them.

Of all the important learnings we have gained, one of the most important is the fact that some humans have a special talent for understanding how to cause and/or adapt to change. Some of these individuals also have the ability to help others learn the sequences of steps that will produce a similar success. People who have these unique skills and serve in this role have been called shamans, educators, teachers, instructors, trainers, coaches, ministers, pastors, lawyers, psychiatrists, psychologists, therapists, social workers, helpers, consultants, and no doubt by many other titles.

If they are really effective at what they do, these change artists help others see themselves and their relationships with the world more accurately and recognize the ways in which they want to change those relationships. Those who want to change their lives will need to act differently to cause the changes they desire. Change artists can help them see how. They can then help the others develop and practice those new behaviors.

Human beings seek change for one reason: they are uncomfortable. It might be the concrete discomfort of a rock in our shoe or the more abstract discomfort of a Michelangelo, who could not rest until he had expressed in marble his vision of human significance and emotion in the Pieta. One of the biggest challenges we face in causing change is that we don't know how to think about the new conditions we want to bring about in our lives clearly or differently enough to produce a new result. The other is that we don't know how to correspondingly change our actions. Usually both of these problems can be solved if we can see more clearly what we're doing now. Thus we need a mirror.

If we want to learn to brush our teeth better, the bathroom mirror will work fine. If we want to learn to drive a golf ball we can use a video recording of how we golf compared to someone like Tiger Woods. But what if we are trying to learn how to influence the people on our IT team to collaborate on developing a new software application, and we've never learned how to guide and inspire and discipline other people effectively?

Then the kind of mirror we need will be someone who does have those interpersonal skills, who can help us discover how to think and feel about the change we seek and how to create that result. We need a coach who is skilled in responsive awareness, someone who can become aware of our emotions and respond to all levels of our behavior (cognitive, emotional, and spiritual as well as physical). This person can help us find our path to the new way of being in the world we are seeking.

To do this, the coach will have to accurately sense our feelings, and intuit or deduce what those feelings mean within the factual situation in our life. This process is what uncovers the personal values that motivate all our action. How does the coach do this? That is what this chapter is all about, and because our work draws heavily from the communications model we describe here, you may want to clarify how this differs from other coaching approaches.

When you, the coach, are serving in this mirroring capacity, you first listen with exquisite care using all your senses and intent. After noticing what you see and hear and feel, you begin to respond in a reflective manner, checking to ensure that you really do understand all the concerns your client is speaking from. You do this by offering your most refined observation of your client's behavior (again this includes cognitive, emotional, spiritual, *and* physical), but because the emotions are by far the most powerful dynamic, you start there. Reading your client, David's, nonverbal behavior (especially his tone of voice) you might offer the reflection: "You feel upset."

You do not ask, "Do you feel upset?" because that is a cognitive question and trying to answer it will shift the client's awareness from the emotional resonance of his limbic brain to a completely different set of circuits in the neocortex that manage linguistic definitions. As a result David will lose his awareness of the emotional state at the center of the discomfort that is directing his need for change. The limbic brain is the center that processes all of our nonverbal behavior. It has been interpreting emotions from facial expression, posture, hand gestures, and commonality for millions of generations of primate behavior. It will make these interpretations available to the cerebral cortex for translation into language, and the two can work together beautifully, but for the cortex to second-guess the limbic brain is just plain rude. That's why you reflected: "You feel upset."

One of the most remarkable things we do as human beings is to label the things and conditions and feelings in our lives in a precise enough manner to track and recall hundreds of thousands of distinctions. If the reflection we offer our clients in the carefully chosen form above does not fit, they will correct us! (If we have been congruently demonstrating respect.)

"No, actually, I don't feel upset as much as confused," David might tell you. "Alright," you respond, "you feel confused." "Yeah," he resumes , "because when I'm standing there Frank tells me he knows how to program in C++ but later Sandra complains that he's continually asking her for help."

Now to continue your role of mirroring your client's experience, you also reflect the cognitive meaning he has just provided and connect the two together. Mirroring his nonverbal behavior (especially his tone of voice), you say: "You feel confused because he says one thing to you in person, but when you're gone, he doesn't follow through." *This helps your client stabilize enough of his experience consciously that he can go further and explore more of what has previously been too abstract to hold in his awareness!*

"Yeah," David jumps in, "and you're right, it *is* upsetting!"

This simple interaction has helped your client establish coherence between two brain systems that can easily be in conflict. The limbic brain actually manages the powerful emotional energy that expresses all the variations of desire, fear, and anger. After the fact, the cerebral cortex composes insightful symbolic associations about why things happened the way they did. We virtually ensure a communication failure when we confuse the very different kinds of "reasons" given by these two very different brains!

The meaning that the client offered in his explanation (paraphrased "because Frank says he knows C++, but he's always bugging Sandra for help") integrates the *feelings* of confused and upset with the *facts* of Frank's *behavior*. Here the coach is not offering cerebral speculation about a linear cause-and-effect analysis, but reflecting the shorthand description of the client's internal state that *he* provided, *in his own language!* Using the client's own words is the essence of respect, and that lies at the heart of responsive awareness.

Understanding and practicing this model will significantly help your clients to build Responsive Awareness.


## EMOTIONAL LITERACY

Emotional literacy, as we work with it at Collaborative Growth, has three components:

1. Reading yourself—that's using your personal awareness of how you feel and the limbic brain's "why" of what is giving rise to those feelings
2. Reading others—that's using your capacity for empathy and developing relationships throughout key parts of your life

3. Reading the environment—that's doing a reality check to determine whether you are responding accurately and using all the key information available in choosing your emotional and strategic responses.

As you work with your clients to build their capacity for emotional responsiveness, it will be essential to build every aspect of their emotional literacy. We discuss expanding their skills in reading themselves and others later in this chapter and in Chapters Three and Four. First, let's explore reading the environment, which means we add accurate context to information before we respond. It also means strategically picking up on critical information. Another way of describing this skill is political savvy. Applying this capacity often needs illumination, especially if our client is emotionally charged about a situation.

We know that each individual's perception about what happens in a situation will genuinely differ and working with this complication is a vital part of effective listening. We evaluate any situation based on all of our life's experience, our values, and our lexicon of emotions. Thus, if Jose is angry with Patty because of the way she wrote a report, you need to help Jose unpack the situation to calibrate the appropriateness of his response. On one hand, you may want to work with Jose to understand whether his and Patty's expectations were the same and whether the difference in format or content is actually compromised. Is it a difference in style or an important difference in how they are communicating a message that others will rely on?

At another level, rather than directly discussing his response to Patty, you might focus on assisting Jose to recognize how and why he is responding the way he is. Is he managing his emotions so he gains the best personal benefit and respect in his relationships or, for example, is he complaining to you but meek at work? Either path of inquiry can be valuable to address, depending on your client. It is important for you as the coach to pay attention to how you guide the exploration, knowing that you have choices.

Marie exhibited an interesting combination of resignation and hopefulness when she described the latest vignette in her career. She is an extremely bright woman, a graduate of excellent schools, and full of capability. Yet she was sidetracked in her career as a federal executive and ultimately ended up in an okay senior position where she knew she was giving value, but which really didn't capture her passion. Then, wham, she was moved to a meaningless job to make way for a young political appointment. She's looking at two and a half years of just marking time until she qualifies for retirement unless she can come up with some other strategy.

Marie sought a coach to help her work through this challenge. She just couldn't imagine going to a meaningless job for even a day, much less for years. Yet she couldn't give up her retirement income. She and her family rely on it.

Marie's coach listened, helped her widen her lens in understanding her responses to the situation and then to craft her actions and upgrade her self-talk, which greatly improved her self-regard. Through Marie's story and many others that we hear, we have the opportunity to listen with the ears of our heart, to guide awareness through open-ended, curious questions, and to help our clients develop responses based on full awareness.

Marie reported that at one point her coach said to her: "What do you expect? This is Washington, D.C.!" This straightforward observation/question released Marie. Strategic and political job moves happen all the time in that world, she knows it, and now it happened to her. It's time for her to find another alternative, be it another position or to negotiate an early retirement. Be careful in the questions you ask as a coach; they can focus your clients' understanding of the situation—for better or worse. Helping to conduct a reality check with the appropriate questions can help them sort out the validity and practicality of their emotional responses. That reality check is key to reading the environment.

## MOTIVATION TO RESPOND

Something within us insists on having a reason for moving, for taking action. That's a good thing, as it is the lynchpin for purposeful behavior. Yet it's often a fairly complex process to understand the reasons why we act. A central role for the coach is to help your clients uncover the reason why to do or not do something and how to respond to their particular emotions. From an internal perspective, the need for purposeful behavior may be as important as having enough oxygen is to a fire at the external level. Choices abound. We can choose to be happy or bored; we choose our attitude and whether to ask for new opportunities. Working with our clients to understand and possibly to find motivation may be one of the most important roles of a coach—and it is undoubtedly relevant to responding with awareness.

As a concept, motivation is a term used to describe what it is within an individual that arouses, maintains, and channels thoughts, feelings, and behaviors. Motivation serves to spark intentions, to develop goals, to make us aware of the purpose for a desired action. In fact, there is a direct neurological link between our motivation and our actions; the only question is whether we're aware of our motivation. Transpersonal psychologists such as Carl Rogers and Abraham Maslow believed that all individuals have a drive for self-actualization, which is a central motivator for taking action. This concept is explored in Chapter Seven on Authentic Success. To feel that congruence of authentic success, we must begin by learning to act with responsive awareness.

Ask your clients, "What's in it for you to ___" [fill in the blank with whatever you're exploring be it emotions, thoughts or actions]. Thus, "What's in it for you to feel so unhappy with your work?" The insightful answer might be: "The unhappiness is getting me to move toward applying for a new job. I'm sick of this!"

Paying attention can be hard work, and there's a wide variety of choices of what to pay attention to, so the more clarified your client's motivation is, the better possibility he or she will have of gaining valuable insights and deciding on the most effective responses. As a coach, if you take on the intention of helping your client expand his or her awareness (and we hope you do take this on), you will be compelled to work with motivation. The purpose of any action develops a screen around what we do and don't notice and what we do and don't respond to. The goal of being aware is to gain increasingly accurate and more comprehensive data—both emotional and cognitive. It's both being able to widen our own lens as we evaluate what's happening and being able to shift and make an informed assessment of what others in the interaction would see through their lenses, and how they would respond.

Motivation is always an extension of the values we're deciding to act on. Thus, clarifying the impetus and the connection to the values motivating your clients' choices and behavior—be it a vote for fun, family, or finances— will inform their awareness and promote even more effective responses.

# AWARENESS OF HOW YOU FEEL AND WHY

Our emotions are so central to any action we take that a lack of understanding how we feel is tantamount to deciding to build a bridge without any awareness of the materials that will be used. Our emotions are a central part of every action and every decision. They can't be eliminated, but they can be ignored at the conscious level. An important opportunity for you, the coach, is to help your clients become accurately aware of their emotions. The word "accurately" is important and is closely connected with our clients' emotional vocabulary as well as their willingness to honestly assess events.

Have you met anyone whose whole emotional vocabulary consists of only three words—sad, mad, and glad? A limited vocabulary is a reflection of limited awareness. Recognizing nuances makes a big difference. There are lists of hundreds of emotions you can share with your client. Perhaps you could challenge him or her to discern ten new emotions in one of your meetings. Some will actually be new; many will turn out to be familiar words but ones that your client doesn't use. Adding this nuance of emotional distinctions can create clarity. For example, in deciding how important it is to take action, it matters whether the emotion felt is distraction or amazement.

Robert Plutchik (2001) wrote an article on emotions in which he presents a wheel of emotions that shows increasing levels of engagement along the same emotional continuum. For example, instead of just sad, choices could increase from pensiveness, to sadness to grief. Instead of mad, choices could be annoyance, anger, or rage. Instead of glad, the continuum he posits is serenity, joy, and ecstasy. Of course, there are many other emotions that fit in those categories. Clarity is essential because it guides how we choose the appropriate response. When we're feeling annoyed, we might just decide to let something go; however, rage requires action.

Gaining a bit of personal insight into one's emotions makes a big difference because it helps our clients understand how much they really care. This requires that you as the coach need a wide range of emotions available to you to be able to best serve your clients. For example, what if your client has a habit of complaining about something, yet once he or she recognizes that it is only an annoyance, can finally drop it and focus on what's more important. The converse can happen as well. Let's say René mentions in passing that she wishes she'd received the promotion that Jenny got, and then says, "Oh well, that's life." Just as she starts to go to another topic, you guide her to stay with the event of not receiving the promotion. Reflect with her about what's she's feeling and why—in that deepest limbic sense we have described. Keep going with her on this journey of investigation, knowing that her first answers are not likely to reach the full truth for her. You might ask questions about which of her values are affected by this decision. It could be that she really wants to develop her career and now she feels blocked. Or it could be that she was worried the new job would take far too much time and interfere with her parenting time, so now she's actually relieved. René could discover she never really wanted the job or that she cares a lot more than she was letting herself know. Either way, this is important clarification that will provide real value to René. With this information in hand, she now has the ability to move toward responding appropriately. Without it she'd be missing the mark.

The "why" of how we're feeling is vital information. Without knowing what has triggered a response, how can we respond with any accuracy? This will take a willing search during your coaching sessions. Often people develop habits of categorizing their responses to events. Their conversation may be something like: "Oh, he's just grouchy in the morning. I don't have to respond much to my teammate, even though I really don't like the way he's treating me." Or it could be "I wish I could go to my daughter's ball games, but it's not in the cards, so I just do my work." The first scenario could mean that the individual is ignoring critical information from a teammate and really should act. By paying attention to that awareness of disliking the treatment from the teammate, your client could recognize this relationship has moved from a bit antagonistic to really hostile. It will bring the team's productivity and certainly the team spirit down if the two don't deal with this challenge. In this scenario, taking aware action will be important to many people.

In the second scenario, your client, Jake, could be right that he just can't get time off, but by paying attention to his feelings and what's triggering it he might notice that he really is spending very little time with his daughter. This awareness can help him find another time when he can be with her. Without action, she could grow resentful, he might start just accepting an unacceptable outcome, and their whole relationship could be impaired. Be careful to ask open-ended questions and leave most of the talking time to your client, but do help connect the actual emotions with the triggering event.

Often we use a simple yet powerful phrase to help our clients connect what they're feeling with what it means to them and to help others they are communicating with fill in the missing blanks for themselves. This wisdom emanates from the excellent communications work of Robert Carkhuff (1971). Here again is the phrase that encapsulates the process we discussed at the beginning of the chapter and the deep work we've been illustrating. Once you have established limbic resonance with your client you can use to great benefit the phrase: "You feel_____ because_____."

When your clients have grown familiar with the emotional side of what this language pattern is capable of expressing, you can ask them to apply the strategy to themselves, to check in on what feelings they are aware of and what is giving rise to those feelings by filling in the blanks for "I feel_____, because_____." In other coaching approaches, the approach might be, "I feel_____. What matters to me about this is:_____ This emotion opens these possibilities for action_____ and closes these possibilities for action_____." Connecting these two parts of awareness are what promote right action that is responding well.

## REFLECTIVE PRACTICES

### Mirroring

One of the most powerful ways to expand our emotional awareness is to use reflective practices. Reflection uncovers multiple meanings. One vital form of reflecting, particularly in coaching, is using reflection as a process of mirroring. How else can we possibly understand how we show up except through receiving information back from others? Your clients' awareness increases when they receive a reflected image of how their conversation sounds, how their actions look, and how their energy or attitude feels. Often your clients create their own mirrors by listening to themselves with openness during a coaching session. They may suddenly recognize new perspectives about the stories they are telling themselves. After listening to themselves for a while with the aid of your open questions, they could decide the situation is really not that important, silly even, or of much greater consequences than they had realized and they'd best act—now. The mirroring is developed by your engagement as a coach, as well as their process of listening with finer attunement.

## Fast Forward

We often think of reflective practices as taking time to write in a journal or talk to a coach. In essence, it includes the process of reconsidering previous actions, events, or decisions. Reflecting can have a fast forward component as well. For example, you could imagine it's six months down the road, you did take the action you're thinking about. How well is it working for you? What's working well? What's askew? The purpose is to gather a sense of whether to take the action under consideration and, if so, to discover how to tailor your course of action.

## Strategies

There are many ways of building emotional awareness through powerful reflection. Strategies include:

- Intentionally acknowledging emotions, attitudes, thoughts, and actions in writing or conversations.
- Expanding one's emotional vocabulary, for example, have a list of emotional words you don't usually use and intentionally put them in sentences a few times through the week. You might begin with apathetic, bewildered, expectant, righteous, poetical, or tranquil just for fun.
- Expand your somatic awareness. What's your body telling you? There are many common references to body talk, such as "My shoulders are tight because I'm so worried about. . . " or "I have a nervous stomach; I'm so excited about this big presentation." If you work interactively with your body, you will be amazed at how much you will learn.
- Use the phrase, "I feel ___ because __" with yourself and others and pay attention to what you're saying from all parts of your brain—your feelings and your analytical processing.

Specific ways you might reflect include:

- Journal writing—even if only a few minutes several times a week
- Take a walk in nature and Think Things Through, it's using the Triple T that Marcia writes about in her book, *Life's 2% Solution* (2006).
- Discuss your concerns openly with a coach, a qualified peer, or a friend.

- Join a group that focuses on the topic of your concern and share with people similarly situated. There's strong evidence that cancer support groups, twelve step groups, bible study groups, and any number of other focused groups provide tremendous help.

## REFLECTING AS A COACH

Being a curious, compassionate, and courageous mirror for your clients is one of the core gifts you can give them. In the mediation training offered by Collaborative Growth, participants spend considerable time in role plays practicing their new skills development. They learn to reflect the concerns, interests, and solutions raised by the people in conflict, generally referred to as the disputants. This act of reflection is not a direct recitation of what's been said, but a paraphrase or summary of key points. It is especially important to notice whether something is mentioned several times or in a heightened tonality, or any other way in which the person is emphasizing a point, even if he or she doesn't consciously recognize it. We'll challenge the mediators to over-reflect during the role play—to reflect more often than seems natural or even respectful. Then when we are debriefing the process we'll ask the disputants how that "over-reflection" felt. As long as it was done sincerely, we've never yet had anyone say it was too much. Try it yourself. Remember to always be respectful, but stretch yourself with willing friends or colleagues to learn how far you can take reflection before it's overdone.

People want to be heard more than they want to be right. You confirm they are heard when you reflect or mirror what they are saying. Through your gift, much of their own internal wisdom can surface. This is the gift of building their awareness. Of course, the ultimate intention must be on their building the skill of paying attention to how they feel and why on their own, as you won't be there most of the time.

## AWARENESS OF THE EMOTIONS OF OTHERS

Responsive awareness includes the key component of understanding the emotions of others. The emotional and social competencies most employed to accomplish this imperative skill are empathy and the willingness and ability to develop long-term friendships that have depth. Action seldom occurs in isolation. The fabric of our social and personally influential networks is vastly more connected than most of us realize. Remember the concept of six degrees of separation?

Thus, as we develop responsive awareness, we must choose our actions in recognition of the impact we have on others. This greatly ups the ante, as the poker term goes. It's tricky work to really understand how we feel; now we're saying it's critical to add in awareness of how others are feeling and why. As with any skill enhancement, the core approach is to develop this capacity one step at a time. In addition to the information here, review Chapter Four on Valuing Others to better understand this essential domain of emotional and social functioning.

The first step in learning empathy is forming the *intention* to pay attention, to notice, and to care how others feel. This means listen, listen, listen. Even if your clients don't appear to be innately compassionate, you can begin by helping them appreciate the powerful business case for paying attention and demonstrating interest in the well-being of those they are seeking to interact with or influence. People are more likely to cooperate with someone if they feel understood by that person and if they feel that person has their best interests at heart. That outcome is increasingly successful for our clients when they understand the emotions of the people they would like to influence and what is motivating their actions. We hope that, upon experiencing success, the positive feelings of giving empathy will begin motivating your client's behavior toward wanting to understand others.

Recognizing what emotions others are responding to comes from paying attention through every channel of awareness that occurs when one:

- Listens!! It's amazing what people will tell you. They may name their emotions directly, such as being enthused, apprehensive, fascinated, or nervous.
- Notices the nonverbal information. Most of our communication is nonverbal and it comes in many dimensions—the speed and tonality in which someone is speaking, how they are standing or sitting, their breathing, their face color, their eyes, mouth, and other parts of their facial expressions. This is rich territory. One good source if you're just getting started in reading facial expressions is Paul Ekman's book

*Emotions Revealed* (2003). He uses many pictures to guide the reader in discerning subtle facial expressions and the feelings that lie behind them.

- Respectfully explore how someone is feeling and then follow up your reflection by inquiring about the reason for the feeling. For example, in a coaching session Catherine eagerly reported her success in better understanding her team leader, Tim. She had felt distant and disconnected from him. She just couldn't figure out how to get on the same page and really feel like a team member.

  In response to coaching guidance, she started asking more about what was important to him and for the team. The team needed to come up with a new strategic plan on their new medical device rollout, and communication was important or they were likely to miss the mark and disappoint the department director. Catherine was highly motivated to improve her capabilities. She was excited to be on the team and wanted to contribute. She just couldn't figure out how. At the next meeting Tim said their draft plan was okay, and they might just have to live with it. Directly indicating her interest, Catherine asked him to tell her more. Tim moaned, saying he had another big project that was late for another team he was on, he was stressed out, and he just couldn't do two projects any more.

  Catherine realized he'd been doing his best not to show his stress. Previously, she had wondered whether he was lazy or just had much lower standards than she did. Now a different picture was developing. She had no idea he was so stressed. She let him know that she empathized and would love to help. Catherine had time to work on their strategic plan. If he'd give her some guidance, she volunteered to do the research and editing.

  This simple interaction was transformative. It was the beginning of a highly collaborative relationship, Catherine became a leading contributor on the team, and Tim's stress was substantially reduced.

- Reflects. This is the next step in the reflecting process for your clients. First you taught them to pay attention to their own feelings and let themselves and others know how they felt with the formula "I feel____ because____." At this stage, the formula is shifted to give others feedback. The beginning of the formula is "You feel____because____." Of course, in the real setting it's important to use the actual emotions in play. Catherine could say, "Wow, Tim, it sounds like you're stressed because you have too much on your plate with two big projects at once." Tim is likely to say, "Darn right, and something has to give." Or he might clarify his emotional state with "Yes, I'm stressed, but mostly I'm worried. I really want to meet our department director's needs and I'm afraid I'll fail on both projects." With this one interaction Catherine now knows he's stressed, cares about quality and about the director. She has considerable information for using her own responsive awareness to build the team's capacity, help Tim have a better life, and feel more satisfied with her contributions.

## RESPONDING WITH EFFECTIVE ACTION

The final step in responsive awareness is to take action. Once we understand how we are feeling and why and have confirming information from others involved, we have much of the emotional and social information needed. The next step is to have the courage and patience to respond with balanced perspective. The following chapters on courage and authentic success will support your coaching to accomplish these goals.

## DEVELOPING RESPONSIVE AWARENESS— COACHING PETRA

The following example of a client's challenge helps demonstrate some of the principles just discussed. Petra was the regional director of a financial services company in New Jersey. Her supervisors were not happy with her performance; neither were many of the employees in the one-thousand-person company. She has just heard she will be transferred to a new position in a few weeks. No one on her staff knows yet, but she's aware many will be glad or relieved. Petra has been very protective of her feelings; as an accountant she never was challenged to use feelings much before. She finds them messy and used to think they were counterproductive. However, she's embarrassed to lose this position and is experiencing enough pain to know something has to change. They will move her to a new position within the company, but she knows she really needs to leave and has been looking for a new job for a while with no success. Here's a summary of one session with her coach:

*Petra:* I've just received the word; I'm being reassigned effective three weeks from today.

*Coach:* Whew, you knew it was coming, but how does it feel now that it's here?

*Petra:* Fine, no problem. I'll just do what I have to do. I know how to suck it up; I'm a professional.

*Coach:* As a professional, you feel you should suck it up, be fine, and move on.

*Petra:* You got it. That's what keeps me going. Just put one foot in front of another.

*Coach:* Petra, that sounds painful. Where is there space for you?

*Petra:* You mean just me? I don't know, uh, I feel kinda squished. . . . .Do I count?

*Coach:* [After waiting to see whether Petra had any more to offer] Yes, Petra, you count. You and your personal feelings are always relevant. Squished is quite descriptive of how you're feeling. Let's talk about that first and consider professional behavior later. [Seeking to get her to be willing to acknowledge her feelings, and keep it safe. It doesn't matter whether she categorizes them as personal or professional, they are her feelings. However, Petra doesn't realize that yet.]

*Petra:* How do I feel, how do I feel . . . .well if we're going there, I feel angry, frustrated, hurt, worried. I don't know . . . it's a jumble churning in my stomach and in my head. [Her face relaxes and she begins to show some of her emotions. Her shoulders slump.]

*Coach:* You have a lot going on right now, you feel angry and frustrated with this forced job change.

*Petra:* Yeah, I am angry. It scares me how angry I feel, and I feel scared about the next job. Geez, can I do anything right? Of course I can, I tell myself, but I don't know.

*Coach:* Petra, it's understandable that you have a lot of feelings right now. This is a big change with a lot of people involved. You're being forced to change jobs and you feel angry. That's a big feeling, and I'm glad you're talking about it. And you're also worried about whether your company will feel you do anything right. [Acknowledging both the anger and the worry and the power situation Petra is dealing with. Her supervisors are unhappy with her performance so they are making her move to a new position, and she's understandably worried about whether they will ever be satisfied with her performance.]

*Petra:* Yeah, I want to focus on the next job and get it right, but my thoughts keep going to what's happened to get me booted out, and I'm just plain angry. It isn't fair. My body's so tight with all this I can't sleep. [Petra's tone is getting louder and louder. She now really sounds angry.]

*Coach:* [In a slightly raised tone as well.] You are a wise woman. You are really noticing what's happening for you. You are angry about this change right now and worried about how to respond in the future. It's kind of hard to manage both at once, so what if we focus on the present for today, and talk about how you feel about being booted out of this job, as you put it? [Guiding her to focus on one aspect, the present, and work with those difficult emotions.]

*Petra:* Suits, me. I do have a lot of emotions about being kicked out. Well but, I do have to get ready for this new position. We can't forget it. I start that in a few weeks.

*Coach:* Let's promise together that we'll get to that new position in a timely manner in another session. Does that feel safe? [Acknowledging the legitimate need to prepare for the new position and make new choices. Also, recognizing there are so many emotions happening that if they aren't sorted out it will be impossible to clarify what emotion belongs where and how to respond, if at all.]

*Petra:* Yes, it's safe, and I'm so blankety blank angry that I just see red. This is unfair. Some of the staff ganged up on me and talked to the supervisors, the supervisors didn't support me enough. And it's true, I guess, I'm a terrible communicator. Nobody knows how I feel. They think I'm made of steel, and I'm not. I care about getting the job done well.

*Coach:* You feel ganged up on and like your supervisors didn't support you. Do they know how you feel?

*Petra:* I just give them the company line. I agreed to take communications training. I'll find out what they want in the new job and just get it done.

*Coach:* And how does your anger play into this?

*Petra:* I'm lost. I don't know. I wish I could tell them how I feel, but I'm scared.

*Coach:* Petra, you've mentioned many feelings today. I'm making a list that I'll give you to work with over the next week. To mention a few, you've talked about anger, frustration, worry, being scared. These are very understandable. You're in the midst of a challenging situation. [Acknowledging the emotions and the difficulties Petra is facing.] You agreed that for the moment you will focus on your present feelings, as you just received word of the transfer. Who can you talk to about how you feel? [Seeking to guide her to talk about and work with her feelings so that later she can communicate the right amount of concern and capability to her supervisors.]

*Petra:* Well I can talk to you, my husband . . . I guess I could talk to a friend. I don't usually talk about how I feel. I just go on. Hmm, I could call Belinda and schedule a long lunch; no, dinner would be better so I don't have to go back to work. And I know William, my husband, is worried. He'd really like me to talk to him more. [She's visibly relaxing a bit.] Yeah, I need to talk about how I feel, it's such a jumble.

*Coach:* I see that you feel it will help to get some of these many emotions off your chest. Here's an idea as you talk with them, use this formula "I feel_____because_____." This will help you begin to connect your feelings with what you care about. Later as we discuss your approach with your supervisors and your new position, we can work this into your everyday life so they can understand how you feel. And you can understand better as well. [Giving her a concrete strategy to work with and reassuring her that her concerns about next steps will be addressed.]

*Petra:* Okay, this helps. I can follow formulas and I would like to understand this jumble.

*Coach:* Great, Petra, you are wonderful to work with. You're really noticing what's going on. To make even more sense of this jumble, would you take this list of emotions I've written down that you mentioned today and write about them? Take at least fifteen minutes every day, or more if you like. There is so much happening that writing about it will help get those feelings expressed, out of your body, and a few may be ones to take action on. You can bring your notes to our next meeting.

*Petra:* Hmm, well, I am busy and writing takes time. Oh, what am I saying? My whole career is in a churner. I have to learn from this. Yes, I'll write and bring in my notes. What else? I'll do anything.

*Coach:* [Gently chuckling] You are a real go-getter. I see your potential shining through. Let's not overload your plate. Take care of yourself, get some exercise. My experience is that the challenges of life work out. Do you have that experience, Petra?

*Petra:* Well, yeah. They do. This is just one of the hardest I've faced.

*Coach:* Yes, it's big for you. So let's end today by letting the energy flow in your body. I find that deep breaths can be a great releaser. Let's breathe. [Exhaling and inhaling slowly so she can be heard to guide Petra in doing the same.]

Petra did the deep-breathing exercise and left with her body a bit more flexible and a plan for acting in the present by learning more from the many emotions she's experiencing.

In this chapter, we identified the four components to responsive awareness and connected those with the practice of emotional literacy, which entails your reading yourself, others, and the environment. We discussed strategies for increasing awareness, including when you, as the coach, mirror your clients' emotions and help them connect those emotions with their cognitive explanations about the matter you're working on. Connecting the emotions your clients are feeling with their explanations promotes their ability to respond with power and to make more consciously aware choices. We discussed provided strategies for building emotional awareness such as through reflective engagement. We discussed building awareness of the emotions of others through building skills in empathy and interpersonal awareness, which connects with the discussion in Chapter Four on valuing others.

*Too busy explaining life, we forget to listen to it.*
*Most of all, we forget to love life.*

# CHAPTER 6

# Courage

Courage is the emotion that allows us to act on what matters to us, in the presence of danger, difficulty, uncertainty, or pain, accepting that there will be consequences without necessarily knowing what those will be but acting anyway, without being stopped by fear or being sidetracked from our chosen course of action.

In this chapter we will consider courage as a fundamental ingredient in the many different kinds of change processes your clients undertake. It is a critical key to sustaining motivation, and this makes your ability to help them develop courage of the utmost importance. Personal growth, reorganizing a team, developing a new product, and merging organizations are all normal processes in the workplace, and they all meet some level of resistance. When that resistance becomes sufficiently intense, succeeding will require courage. We explore several specific ways of being courageous: the courage to speak, the courage to act, the courage to trust, and the courage to test our own version of reality.

It is true that humans come pre-wired with some survival strategies, such as avoiding high places from which we could fall, but it is also true that the fear and cautiousness that help us survive in an uncertain and increasingly complex world are *learned* responses to unknown or potentially painful experiences. Courage gives us the ability to act against past experience when it warns that something could be dangerous and painful, either physically or emotionally. It strengthens your clients' determination and focuses their desire to help them move in the direction of achieving their goals anyway. When they are stuck and can't or won't act on behalf of their self-actualization, no matter how badly they may want to, you can help them increase their emotional effectiveness by developing courage.

To understand courage we must understand what it is that so often prevents it. At a physiological level, the largest obstacle we face is pain. Our bodies are small, and weak, and tender in comparison to many of the enormous tasks we require ourselves to perform. No matter how big and tough they may seem to us, they are not immune to time and gravity and the psychological stress and pressures that can wear them out from the inside. To some extent we know all this and take obvious steps to see to it that our bodies are kept as safe and comfortable as possible.

But there are also other obstacles that prevent us from achieving the goals we cherish and hope to attain. Loss, rejection, loneliness, or just the fear of these consequences can halt our progress, to the point at which we stop working and refuse to make any further efforts. In this sense courage is an ally of desire that you as a coach must be able to help your clients enlist on behalf of their self-actualization. When they are not able to want what they want with sufficient intensity to obtain it or at least persist in the effort, you can help them buttress their motivation and increase their chances of success if you can help them "Take courage."

## PATIENCE, ENCOURAGEMENT, AND INDEPENDENCE

It is certainly no mystery why pain prevents us from achieving our goals. When it hurts physically to move, to focus and sustain our attention, to communicate empathically and respectfully with others, it is very hard to be effective. All we want to do is retreat, allow our bodies to relax and heal, to nurture them and eliminate all the demands on us. Working in pain is exhausting; it requires an enormous amount of our energy to direct our attention toward our work and to resist the demands for attention from the injured location.

When your clients are dealing with this sort of challenge, the kind of courage that they need will often be the courage to be patient. In these times when irrationally long schedules are the norm, the pain of injury or disease might just be "nature's way of telling you, Something's wrong!" But that does not mean your clients will not resent the "opportunity" and that they will not "kick against the pricks" of their condition. It takes courage for them to be able to re-examine their priorities and perhaps even relinquish some of the goals which they cherished, but, given the strength of their bodies, were unrealistic. Coaching for patience and acceptance and detachment are the remedies indicated here.

But what about when the pain is more subtle? What if it is the painful memory of a failure or a loss that is preventing their forward motion? When your clients are afraid of repeating a mistake or re-experiencing some kind of loss, the goal of your coaching is to encourage them—to build their faith in themselves and their abilities as well as in their capacity to recover from adverse circumstances. Encouragement coaching includes helping your clients regain control of the rate at which they attempt to process reality—that may be one day at a time, one hour at a time, or maybe just what's happening now. Then, when life is coming at them at a more manageable speed, they can begin rebuilding the size of the vision and giving it detail and concrete parameters once again, but not too little . . . not too big . . . just right! Your clients may need to build their strength in a safe environment in which they can test it and increase their confidence without being on the front lines risking everything.

Fear of rejection is one factor influencing the exercise of courage. How many of your clients do you think are afraid to speak in public? According to the statistics they *all* are, except for about 20 percent of that one guy who's always such a showoff. People are afraid to speak in public because we are social creatures who are hardwired to avoid rejection, and the best way to do that is to not rock the boat and go along with the crowd. The problem is that very frequently the crowd does not have your client's unique best interests at heart. They can't, because they don't even know he or she exists. For the most part, the crowd moves according to collective pressure and in rare instances to the extremely persistent and focused pressure of single individuals. You could find yourself in a coaching conversation where your client may have the perfect solution to the biggest problem in the organization, but if he or she is not able to advocate for him- or herself and that solution effectively, it will never be noticed, let alone implemented.

The courage to make decisions based on the criteria your client has determined to be most relevant is central to their skill in the emotional competency called independence in the Bar On EQ-i. The fear of being rejected (and the similar fear of being lonely) work against your clients' independence, and in order to be able to help them speak up for themselves you will need to help them develop of the ESE strategy of courage. This may include some instruction in relaxation techniques to help override some of the body's biological programs, and it will *certainly* include exploring which kinds of assertive behavior will best express the emotional energy and passion that connects them to what matters most. This can be making decisions as simple as avoiding the Asian food they dislike in favor of the Italian they love, or as complex as deciding where and when to retire and what kind of supports will need to be in place for them to enjoy the "golden" years of their lives in the way they prefer.

## THE COURAGE TO SPEAK

Needing the courage to speak up and voice our preferences or opinions in the workplace is a familiar experience. For some people even this much "public speaking" is uncomfortable. In any group of people, there will generally be a variety of opinions about the best way to solve the problems of their current life conditions. If your clients want their ideas to be heard and discussed and realized, they will need to demonstrate some courage.

Because we are such social creatures, humans feel a huge need to belong, to be welcomed, accepted, and appreciated by the group. Back in the early days of homo sapiens, being unpopular and not belonging could have a very negative effect on how well you ate, how comfortable your life was, and the likelihood that you would produce descendents who survived. Below the surface of our conscious awareness, these are all things we are preprogrammed to care about very deeply and, because we are all descended from descendents who survived, we enjoy the benefits of a very long genetic memory!

However, the courage to oppose popular opinion is also a valuable survival trait *for society*. While popular opinion usually seeks to preserve the status quo, the ability to consistently adapt to change is the preeminent feature of success in human history. As we have grown more and more civilized (read: complacent) it turns out we resist a lot of what is in our long-term best interests because in the short term, processing change is both psychologically and biologically uncomfortable.

There will be times when your clients know something they need to say in order to be congruent with themselves, but they will find it very difficult, if not impossible to do so. Because you are the coach and will not be directly affected by the information, they may find that it is possible to discuss the matter with you, and you will have the challenge and opportunity to help them develop that kind of courage. There is another kind of courage that shows up when your clients aren't yet clear about what they need to address. If they are feeling too troubled by some issue to investigate it in much depth, you may need to create enough safety for them to approach the problem indirectly without discussing the content per se. Courage is a step-by-step unfolding.

In the first situation it may be very challenging to avoid expressing a personal opinion of what you think is right for them to do. Honestly, you may not be able to avoid developing your opinion, but the practice of good coaching requires that you avoid announcing your decision and thus polluting the evolution of their personal reflective process. Your clients will only be able to develop their own emotional intelligence to the extent that *they* get to explore their situation, test out *their* hypotheses about life, and make their own mistakes. When they seem headed in the direction that could be less than fully successful, sometimes the best you can do is to help them consider consequences they may not have foreseen. The elegance of your coaching for reality testing will make a big difference.

In the second situation, you can still help your clients develop their courage, even though they may seem to be keeping you at arm's length (or further). In a situation like this, here is how we proceeded:

*Client:* It's definitely not anything I feel comfortable sharing with anyone.
*Coach:* So you're the only one who knows about this concern you have?
*Client:* That's right, I'm the only one.
*Coach:* And from what I think I heard you saying earlier, it is very uncomfortable not being able to share this information with others.

*Client:* Absolutely, you've got it.

*Coach:* What would happen if this information got out?

*Client:* I guess that depends on who learned of it.

*Coach:* So just for an experiment, write down the names or initials of the five people from whom you most want to protect this information.

*Client:* Okay. [Client thinks and writes for a couple minutes, then looks up.]

*Coach:* So now write down what each one of these people would have to say to you if he or she learned you knew this and were keeping it from them. Take your time.

*Client:* Okay [this time the client writes for about ten minutes before looking up to indicate that he's through.]

*Coach:* Do you think that you have pretty accurately guessed their responses? How does it feel for them to hypothetically know the secret you've been guarding?

*Client:* Very chaotic and freaky. I feel nervous, as if they already know. I'm so uncertain what might happen next!

*Coach:* So it sounds like you're already having some of the emotional responses you would have if this information were really public?

*Client:* [Pausing] Yeah, I guess I am, but don't think for one minute that this clever trick is going to get me to tell them.

*Coach:* It's not a trick, and I don't have any investment in which way you choose. I respect that this is your life.

*Client:* Yeah. . . .

*Coach:* But just for fun, add my name to the list and write down what you think I'd say too.

*Client:* Okay [he writes for a few minutes and looks up].

*Coach:* So now characterize the feelings of each of these people in one word and write that beside the name or number or whatever you've got. [This will cause the client to tap very deeply into empathy and emotional awareness skills.]

*Client:* [After a few minutes he looks up.] Okay.

*Coach:* So now in one word write down how you feel about the fact that they feel that way.

*Client:* This is going to be tough!

*Coach:* Maybe, but you might be surprised, so give it a go, and let's see.

*Client:* Okay. [After less than a minute] I'm done.

*Coach:* That went faster than I thought. Does that mean it's pretty clear to you?

*Client:* Yeah, that part really is.

*Coach:* So what, if any, value have you received from going through these pretty simple exercises that really left your secret intact?

*Client:* I realize I've got some serious work to do! I haven't been letting people know what really matters to me or how I really feel about it.

*Coach:* And that's caused some real snarls in these relationships. . . .

*Client:* No doubt! This is very intense, no doubt, but it's different than I imagined.

*Coach:* Interesting. In what way?

*Client:* The people who matter most are eventually going to be able to deal with this, and I think they will stay in my life. The people who aren't going to get over it are the ones who don't know who I am. They think I'm the person I've sort of been pretending to be in order to keep things comfortable and accommodate a lot of expectations that I believed I had to live up to, so of course they couldn't understand my decisions.

*Coach:* Wow, I get it. So where do we go from here?

*Client:* I don't know. It's not like I'm going to go out and tell everybody what they really don't want to know this afternoon.

*Coach:* Okay.

*Client:* First, I've got to figure out how to quit selling out on what matters most to me.

*Coach:* Can you do that?

*Client:* I've got to! I'm going to . . . yeah, somehow I can.

*Coach:* Do you want to?

*Client:* Oh yes, more than anything!

Helping your clients develop the courage to speak may require that they grow new roots that tap deeper into their existential nature beyond the masks and conventions of society. That may require a lot of time, or it may not. It may simply require someone like you being willing to encourage them to consider that option as a valid invitation. Mother Nature has given our species a variety of gifts to help us avoid repeating strategies that are no longer relevant to the challenges we are encountering in our life conditions. Courage is certainly one of them!

The coaching process illustrated above in which the specific content of the client's situation remained undisclosed is called content-free coaching and was first developed in the methods of neuro-linguistic programming.

## THE COURAGE TO ACT

Although speech is definitely a powerful form of action, acting courageously often goes a step beyond speaking courageously. If one of your clients is having trouble taking action, an effective coaching invitation might be to have him or her think for a moment and recall the most dramatic image of courageous action he or she can remember. We invite you to do this yourself. After you read the next few sentences, see what comes to mind for you. What do you think back to when you seek to remember an act of courage that you witnessed or heard recounted? It could be something you saw in real life, saw reported on television, or in a movie. What do you feel now as you remember the sights and sounds that gave rise to those feelings?

Tapping into your own recollections of people being courageous and reinvigorating them will help you coach others more effectively.

One very powerful example many people can recall was the young man in Tiananmen Square who attempted to use his body to block the passage of a Chinese tank when the demonstrations for democracy were occurring in Beijing in 1989. Such examples of courageous action usually elicit some kind of a physical sensation in us, a tightening of our stomachs, a clenching of the teeth, a tingling sensation in our skin, something that means *our* bodies know that *their* bodies are in some kind of danger. Probably our most frequent encounter with these kinds of scenes is on television or in the movies, so next time you're observing a situation in which someone is acting courageously, notice what kind of sympathetic resonance your own body undergoes. Making this kind of information conscious develops your somatic awareness, or more accurately liberates it from the realm of the unconsciousness. The more intimately we are in touch with what our own body is telling us, the more helpful we can be to our clients in this exploration.

It is often our idealistic beliefs about what is right and good that inspires and empowers us to act in ways that could endanger our physical safety, or it could be the sheer intensity of our desire that moves us into dangerous territory. Courage to the primitive human included actions like attempting to swim across a treacherous river in order to get to the hunting grounds or the food supply or safety from their enemies that was offered by the opposite shore. Courage is not just a gauge of our relationship with power; it is also an expression of our need and determination to improve those life conditions that impose limitations we feel are unacceptable or even intolerable.

So if you are coaching clients who need to speak or act with courage, how should you proceed? One highly effective strategy is to help them access their own most vivid memories of when acting courageously was powerfully rewarding for them. This requires much more than just remembering a verbal description, it means reactivating as many of the sensory details as they can. Where were they standing? In what posture? What were the sounds and the colors in the environment? How did they feel to be there? Were they hopeful, or nervous, or angry? What were they probably saying to themselves internally in such a situation?

In addition to helping them re-access those memories and that state of courage, help them get in touch with what it was that mattered so much to them that they took action in spite of their fears. When they connect with what truly matters most to them, taking courageous action to achieve it will come much more easily and naturally.

Directly experiencing these images and sounds and tensions and ideas from memory will help them compose the new ingredients needed for their current courageous action! When you as a coach help them re-access these resources in the present, they will feel and understand very precisely the contours of the targets they are seeking to hit. Remembering their way back into these physiological states and conditions will enable them to know what courage is throughout their bones, musculature, and all of their senses in such a way that they can then spontaneously reproduce it! One way to guide your clients into this kind of "remembering" might be with a question like: "When has acting courageously paid off powerfully for you in the past? What compelled you to take action? When did you realize you were being courageous?" By requesting specific detail about the highlights of their stories, you will help them revitalize the mental and emotional states that gave rise to their successes in the past.

If it sounds to you as if they felt brave, for instance, you can strengthen and confirm that experience by saying: "So you felt brave when you confronted your teacher, because no one else had ever stood up to him before." If brave isn't quite what your client felt, he or she will correct you. "No, I felt scared then, but later looking back on it I was surprised at how much courage it took to challenge him." The label he or she chooses for the experience has nothing to do with some absolute state of "courage," "bravery," or "feeling scared" per se. Each of these words merely serves as a unique stimulus for accessing different emotional states and all of the memories and neurological conditions associated with them. Most often it happens unconsciously! The coach has no attachment to what words the clients use—it's *their* state! You can help them evoke whatever states they need in order to discover what emotional ingredients made up their experiences, here for example, bravery.

You're facilitating this allows them to deeply refresh and reinforce the sensory experience *and the emotional significance* of acting bravely, but if you ask them a question like, "Did you feel brave?" you will send them down the path of linguistic rather than emotional exploration, because that form of questioning prompts the mind to analyze the definition of "brave" in comparison with other synonyms and antonyms, rather than accessing the emotional and physiological state that *is* bravery in them.

Our experiences of courage are stored holographically in our physiology as visual, auditory, and kinesthetic information, not just as verbal descriptions, and the more intimately we can help our clients re-access these, the more familiar they will become with how to energize the processes and pathways that lead to acting with courage. Asking coaching questions that use sensory-based language to elicit information about what they saw and heard and felt in the past or *will* see and hear and feel when they have already reached their goals in the future can connect them with surprising new options in the present.

## THE COURAGE TO TRUST

The fourth type of courage differs from speaking and acting in that it does not require any sort of assertiveness. It relates to your clients' capacity to receive and allow. Those are capacities that facilitate openness and the courage to trust. Although it's possible the risks involved can in principle be physical, trusting others additionally includes emotional risks that are greater than just being misinterpreted or misunderstood. Your client could easily wind up feeling disappointed, betrayed, taken advantage of, or any number of things.

Trust is the ability we need when we are called upon to deal with the potential risks of uncertainty. When dealing with known quantities upon which we can rely, developing trust would obviously be unnecessary. It would already be in place. Trust requires the courage to be vulnerable, to risk being hurt or disappointed, and the willingness to experience possible loss based on your own miscalculations or the assurances of another.

Helping clients develop this kind of courage can be facilitated by helping them learn to check whether their observations of their objective situations concur with the way their co-workers assess them. Applying situational, process, and political savvy—this is what reality testing is. It means focusing on what is really the case and screening out both fantasies and distortions. Are your clients' hopes and expectations based on the same kinds of considerations and analysis of the fact pattern that others who are knowledgeable in this area would consider?

In a more abstract, rational way that does not trigger emotions of fear or pessimism, now is the time to help them consider what the possible worst-case scenarios might be if their hopes do not materialize. It can be productive to imagine what sorts of attitudes and behaviors they might need to exercise in order to deal with disappointment and maintain their motivation. Your clients unconsciously conduct this sort of reality testing, whether they are aware of it or not, but when you help them make the process conscious it will be significantly improved through the incorporation of their cognitive reasoning and your reality testing skills.

Recovering from a disappointment, failure, or loss requires that your clients rebuild the emotional resources that motivate and sustain them through difficult times. Such periods often require that they be able to internally source and recharge their energy, hope, and enthusiasm without the external encouragement that comes with success or the recognition and encouragement of others. The strength of their courage to trust forms a powerful bond with optimism to sustain their intentions long enough to make them manifest.

The point is that just living in the extraordinarily complex world of the 21st century and playing actively at the level of contribution that is most fulfilling for us demands a robust courage! Because our lives are composed of many overlapping networks of relationships, we experience such a high degree of interdependency that trust is no longer optional for us or our clients if we aspire to achieve authentic success. The ability to be known and trusted at this level of intimacy depends on how accurately we can communicate what is important to us, why we care about it, and what we want to contribute.

## YOUR OWN COURAGE

We have been speaking mostly about the importance of you helping your clients develop the emotionally and socially effective strategy of courage, but the importance of you developing it in yourself cannot be over-emphasized. Coaches without courage do not serve their clients. A coach needs courage to generate the conversational space with the client that takes the client out of his or her comfort zone. Coaches need courage so as not to fall into "pleasing" the client with what they think the client wants to hear. Coaches need courage to hold *all* the emotions of clients—their anger, sadness, fear, anxiety, ambition, confusion—without falling into those emotions themselves. A coach needs courage to provoke new thinking and new actions within the client.

Another type of courage that coaches need is the courage to do sufficient reality testing. Do I care enough about this client to keep listening to him and reflecting for him, and challenging him when the very weaknesses that are undermining his authentic success are making my job unpleasant? Am I willing to keep holding her accountable when she is frustrated because she believes she has gone as far as she can and I believe otherwise? Do I know enough about the concrete, technical aspects of the work my clients do to anticipate the unavoidable missteps that could delay or derail them?

Answering these and similar kinds of questions can help you make sure that your reality testing is strong enough to outlast the convenient explanations our clients often give (and believe) at first, before they grow strong enough to embrace the real requirements for change. Our failure to do this will consistently undermine even their best efforts.

# COACHING FOR EMOTIONAL EFFECTIVENESS—COURAGE

In this coaching session sample, we will illustrate how a client named Lawrence begins developing more courage in confronting some of his direct reports who have bent the rules consistently for many years and sometimes broken them. Lawrence manages an IT shop for a federal agency.

*Coach:* You told me that the level of stress you're dealing with has become a real problem for you, in part because you have a hard time confronting your direct reports.

*Lawrence:* That's right. I've got people who do pretty much whatever they want when they want. I've never been good at cracking the whip, and now that we are going to start providing web-based service for our internal customers we are going to have a lot of programming to deliver regularly on a really tight schedule, and these people just aren't used to it.

*Coach:* You sound worried that you're not going to be able to hold their feet to the fire because they have such bad work habits. ["You feel_____, because_____."]

*Lawrence:* That's right; right now half my stress is probably coming from dreading all the confrontations that I am certain to have with the team and with my manager.

*Coach:* How closely do the two of you work together? [Assessing the strength of their relationship.]

*Lawrence:* We've worked together in some capacity for over fifteen years and we've always been on pretty good terms, but he's made it really clear that the pressure is already on him, even though we don't start the conversion for about six weeks. I always meet once, maybe two times a week to discuss my team's progress. He knows the problem I've got with these folks, and my lowest marks in my annual review have been in managing subordinates, so the message is clear I've got to improve.

*Coach:* If you look into the future and imagine that you are a couple weeks into the project, what's one of the first problems you're most likely to face?

*Lawrence:* I'll go around the room in a meeting asking for updates from each pair of programmers and Rick and Denny will be behind everyone else, maybe even a day or more.

*Coach:* How will the team respond when they hear that?

*Lawrence:* Bruce will push back from the table and cross his arms across his chest, Ruthie will shake her head and roll her eyes, and Tom will say something under his breath like, "Here we go again." The rest of them will either look down or glare at me.

*Coach:* It sounds like they know pretty much what to expect.

*Lawrence:* Yeah, 'fraid so.

*Coach:* What would be the single most dramatic thing you could do as a manager that would absolutely astound them all?

*Lawrence:* [Long pause] I could separate Rick and Denny.

*Coach:* [Remaining silent while looking at him with a slightly questioning gaze as if to say, "Hmmm that's interesting, and then what?" You want this totally radical idea Lawrence has come up with to really sink in!]

*Lawrence:* Yep, that would be it. It would be just like that country song when the coward of the county locked the barroom door and took on all the bullies.

*Coach:* [Stay silent until just before he starts to speak, then say] "Well maybe, but who could you possibly pair them up with?" [You have just accepted his hypothesis as plausible *and* distracted him from starting to talk himself out of it [in case that's what he was going to do] by giving him a very realistic problem to solve.]

*Lawrence:* Rick could actually work with just about anybody. He's what I'd have to call a follower, but he's learned a lot of bad attitudes from Denny. That guy, on the other hand, can't work with anybody!

*Coach:* And, as their manager, you have allowed this behavior and poor performance to continue for how many years? [Silence so he can take this in and react to it.]

*Lawrence:* You're right, I know. . . . . I actually inherited this problem and the previous manager never did anything to document it or resolve it. I made the excuse I was too busy learning the ropes at first, but now I just can't tolerate it most of the time. The problem is that, the more I think about it, separating those two would be like dragging a mule up a ladder.

*Coach:* It sounds like you're regretting your decision already. [You call it "your decision" prematurely on purpose, as- this strengthens his identification with his own creative idea and works a little bit like the "take-away" strategy in sales. Now if he has any pride in the value of his thought process, he will virtually have to honor his insight. Remember what we said about people "discovering" the truth and feeling a strong natural allegiance to it.]

*Lawrence:* I'm not regretting it, I'm just regretting that I can't support it.

*Coach:* Would you like to be able to support it?

*Leonard:* Of course I want to be able to support it, but just the thought is totally stressing me out already.

*Coach:* Who else will support it?

*Leonard:* Everyone on the team except Rick and Denny, and whoever has to work with Denny!

*Coach:* What about your manager?

*Leonard:* He will be delighted. He and Denny have never gotten along very well. [Notice that he is describing this as a fact about the future. "He *will* be delighted." This is pretty good proof that accomplishing this change is now the behavioral target Leonard has committed to, whether he is fully aware of it consciously or not!]

*Coach:* Then you'll have enough support if you can just get one more person on board. Are you in?

*Leonard:* Who?

*Coach:* You! You've got to get Leonard on board. He has got to see himself as being able to change his behavior, saying no when he feels no, and being able to say yes in such a way that people not only know he means yes, but they feel inspired to join him. [Shifting person like this can help him adopt the point of view from which "he" is observing "Leonard."] Think of an example of some time when someone did something really courageous that you totally admired and wanted to be like.

*Leonard:* I know it's corny, but that song about the coward of the county has always affected me a lot. It's like I just keep wondering when I will be fed up enough to turn around and face whatever's been chasing me.

*Coach:* Let me ask you, Lawrence, what are you afraid of?

*Lawrence:* If I'm afraid of anything it's that I'll have to keep enforcing these new rules all day long and never get any of my own work done! It's probably just been a choice that was convenient, but I will just about need to hire another person simply to manage their relationship.

*Coach:* It sounds like you've got a whole lot of reasons to change, and only a few reasons not to. Your emotions around this are very powerful, we can both feel it.

*Lawrence:* Oh no doubt, this is it. I've never felt this much energy before. It's like I'm shaking from worrying, or excitement, or something on the inside, but in my mind I still doubt that I'll go through with it.

*Coach:* Just for fun, imagine that something highly unusual has happened and you seized the moment and created a total success. You got Denny paired with another programmer and they get along well enough to be fully productive. No one is confused about the fact that there's a new sheriff in town, so not only does the reduced conflict make it more pleasant for team members to be productive, but they know this is now what's expected of them. How do you feel?

*Lawrence:* Are you kidding? I'd feel fantastic! I feel ten years younger. . . . I feel powerful. . . and effective. [Pausing] I feel like I have control over my own life again then.

*Coach:* Great, Lawrence, that is fantastic indeed! Now say that over again even a little bit louder and really listen to the sound of your voice. You're re-accessing a tremendous source of energy in your life that hasn't been available to you for a long time.

*Lawrence:* Okay. I'd feel fantastic, ten years younger! Powerful and effective, like I have control over my life.

*Coach:* Now show me how you would stand. [Leonard stands up straight and tall, his shoulders back and a pleased if somewhat astonished look on his face.] Now walk the way that you would walk if these hassles were resolved and no longer dragging behind you like an anchor. [He does a little clumsily at first as he attempts to adjust to this new state.] Excellent! Now tell me what sort of excuses and complaints you're going to hear from Denny.

*Leonard:* Denny will be totally freaked. I'm not sure what he will say, but I know what he'll do. He'll probably leave work "sick" that day and we won't see him again until he's figured out some way to obstruct this change from happening.

*Coach:* That sounds pretty passive aggressive to me.

*Lawrence:* Yeah, he does not ever confront things very directly. But then again, I see that neither do I.

*Coach:* One of the critical ingredients in courage is being able to tell people what we like and want more of and what we don't like and don't want more of, but even more central than that is feeling congruent that we have the right to say this! It is a key element of successful leadership to be clear about your wants and expectations of the team and to take action when those wants are not being met. How congruent are you feeling now?

*Lawrence:* This is truly remarkable. I feel like everything is all lined up. I'm not only saying what's true for me, but I'm doing what's best for the team, and they both appreciate my doing so and back me up. At least I hope so.

*Coach:* I think they will, but they are likely to be caught off guard as much as Denny is, and I think you'll have to show some consistency before they feel safe to trust that you mean what you say and are going to enforce it.

*Lawrence:* Yeah, I guess I don't really trust that yet either.

*Coach:* I think you're going to want to talk with your manager a lot about this and see what kinds of suggestions he may have. I'd ask him specifically how he will support you in this.

*Lawrence:* See, I'm not very good at that either.

*Coach:* I understand, but fortunately, we've got a few weeks before this really kicks in. At our next session we can practice how to talk with your manager and communicate what you need from him. In fact, for your homework I'd like you to imagine the conversations you're going to have with each member of the team about how all these changes are going to affect them and how they can best support them.

*Lawrence:* Okay, will do! Thanks. Some of this is really huge!

*Coach:* You're welcome.

In this chapter we considered the role courage plays as a fundamental ingredient in many of the change processes that your clients have, or choose to face. Because it is a critical key to sustaining the motivation necessary for completion and success, your ability to help them develop this courage is essential. We looked at several specific ways of being courageous: the courage to speak, the courage to act, the courage to trust, and the courage to test our own versions of reality.

*We need to recover the soul as the domain of learning.*

# CHAPTER 7

# Authentic Success

To reach a lifestyle that supports our whole self, we must dig deep and find what really drives the choices we make and the messages we give ourselves.

In this chapter we explore the transformative results available when your coaching guides your clients to focus on authentic success. This broad strategy links the first four ESE strategies with this fifth one. We discuss the need to help your clients avoid the perfection trap and to become aware of and discipline their self-talk. We also highlight some of the EI skills that most impact the ability to develop authentic success, a term that might be synonymous with self-actualization. We discuss two of the most important skills to address in your coaching—happiness and optimism. We present several strategies throughout the chapter for strategically working with your clients to grow their authentic success, including developing what we call a 2 percent solution.

Living with a congruent sense of authentic success is a tall order and only possible when embraced as a lifelong journey. Our charts in Chapter One that list the skills that are relevant to each of the five ESE strategies list the most skills under this strategy. In fact, every scale from each of the three measures we highlighted plays a role in the unfolding of this strategy.

# DEFINING AUTHENTIC SUCCESS

Everyone must form his or her own definition of authentic success and periodically evaluate the continuing viability and truthfulness of the standard he or she has set. Interestingly though, the process for forming our sense of what is authentic, what is success, and determining whether we are living in accordance with our own criteria is reliably similar across humanity. The difference between success and authentic success is that the latter attends to what we care about *and* incorporates our values. It's a reflection of the recognition of what is deeply meaningful to us. If well thought through, it's balanced so we aren't asking more of ourselves than is possible or healthy. For example, success might be stated: "I work hard and make a lot of money." If your clients say this, you might guide them to take it up a notch and identify what authentic success actually is for them and they might recognize that they want to work hard because they value the contributions they are making to their organization and to society, because they love to learn, or because they value supporting their families. Any of these may be answers to "What is authentic success?" When your clients can truthfully articulate what true success is, they are reflecting a deep understanding of why they do what they do. We have had clients gain deep recognition by finally connecting the dots in a way that helps them understand why they make the decisions they do today and how that relates to choices they want to make in the future.

## The First Steps

Three action steps will make a big difference in helping your clients understand how they view their own authentic success.

1. Get a good take on what success means to your clients as they start discussing the subject they want to address. You might ask them to write about it before you even talk about it. If they tend to go to one extreme (the tasks of daily life) or the most broad and hopeful (helping solve world hunger), remind them of the other indicators of success they've been talking about. Seek to help your clients create a full picture. It's often a blend of wanting increased success professionally and wanting to contribute to their families, their communities, or to end global warming.

2. Next, guide your clients to take a look at their values—particularly focusing on those that are most important. Have them write these out as well.

3. Now bring the two together. How do their values affect their decisions that guide how they are now leading their lives. Your clients may well find they have values they weren't aware of that are driving today's decisions.

Authentic success is the result of integrating our values with our self-talk, daily decisions, and choices.

## Circle Exercise

Here's an exercise to give your clients:

Ask them to bring in their journals or just give them some paper for the exercise. Then ask them to write a list of the most important parts of their lives, such as career, work, family, friends, church, community, exercise, self-care, or finances. Direct them to list those parts that are important and fairly distinct parts of their lives, not just create a laundry list of what they do. Now have them draw a circle and put each of these words into a slice of pie the size of which reflects how much of their time they now spend on that component. Ask questions such as: Is work in proportion or out of balance with the rest of your life? Is there time for play? Did you even put play in your pie? Then ask them to stop, breathe, and reflect on how they'd like their lives to be and draw that pie. Notice what is different. You can further explore the discussion points raised around your clients' results and then jointly create a transition path that will take them from one pie to another.

Coaching with a focus on authentic success is about working with your clients to clarify and live in harmony with the preferred pie (that's pie number 2). It is about helping them take those actions in their lives that are consistent with what truly matters to them. It is drawn authentically if it incorporates vision and reality testing; it includes hopefulness and boldness, and they pace themselves. Transformation is a process, a journey, not a rush job, and whether it is short or long, the value of all that it encompasses cannot be measured by another person.

# CONNECTING ALL FIVE ESE STRATEGIES

Living with authentic success is one of the largest, most transformative, goals someone can seek. When your clients experience authentic success, they will likely be drawing on all four of the earlier ESE strategies we've just discussed and committing additional clarity and purposefulness to living a meaningful life. Let's review the key points from the first four ESE strategies to begin integrating this lifestyle.

- *Valuing Self:* Many centuries ago, Lao Tzu said: "Knowing others is wisdom; Knowing yourself is enlightenment." When your clients find the tipping point for their own authentic success, they will balance understanding and valuing themselves in the most effective way possible— recognizing and acknowledging both their positive and shadow sides.

  *Valuing Others:* Some of the deepest satisfactions of being a coach come from the many ways in which you are allowed to express your value of others. If they don't already, your clients may also come to share this value out of their recognition that so much of workplace and life success requires shared action. Often deciding whether their goals are accomplished requires mutual evaluation. Some actions that have high potential value can be taken by your clients on their own, such as governing their thoughts and self-talk, and praying or meditating. However, most action happens in a social environment. Assisting your clients in developing this skill is a gift. Benjamin Disraeli knew how to help build a community spirit which supported valuing others. He pointed out that the greatest good you can do for another is not just share your riches but reveal to them their own.

- *Responsive Awareness:* At the heart of true awareness lie our reflective skills. Confucius once taught that there are three ways to gain wisdom: first by reflection, which is noblest; second by imitation, which is easiest; and third by experience, which is the bitterest. In order to help your clients understand what is actually happening in their relationships with co-workers and family members and help them respond appropriately, it is important to help them develop reflective practices that increase their sensitivity and awareness. This kind of personal and organizational awareness increases your clients' capabilities to identify what the real issues and concerns are and to respond effectively. If they are telling themselves stories that are far removed from what is happening, they can't respond authentically. Thus, the accuracy of their awareness is an essential step for building success. Next, the willingness to act is required. Success requires action, liberating themselves from paralysis by analysis, or staying stuck for whatever other reason.

- *Courage:* Authentic success may require that your clients finally "gut up" and make that change they've talked about for so long. It could mean leaving an established career and starting a new path. Or it could be just the opposite, having the courage to stay with a situation that seems suboptimal and fails to fulfill other cherished values. Courage is required to nurture the hope of action, even if that action might create consequences they were not looking for. James Joyce was not one to shy away from risk, as he saw it: *Mistakes are the portholes of discovery!*

## THE PERFECTION TRAP

"I'll be successful when all my debts are paid and my retirement is funded." "I'll be successful when I accept life; however it is, and always have a gentle mood." "I'll be successful when I get the next promotion" (and the next, and the next). Every one of these and similar comments are indicative of what you are likely to hear when you ask people to state their personal definitions of success. These are laudatory goals. However, they aren't necessarily grounded in the present; they may be considerably far off or never obtainable. What constitutes success is always a personal criterion, yet as a coach you can guide your clients to use their emotional and social effectiveness to be realistic, grateful for what's here today, and to accept the multiple dimensions of what's happening without angst, while embracing the willingness to continually work toward improvement. One of the biggest gifts you might share is to help your clients discover new definitions of success as they experience it on a day-by-day basis.

One thing about life is its developmental potential; your clients' capabilities evolve in unexpected ways, and this will be enhanced if they lead their lives with an expectant awareness. Developing that awareness and a context for accurately understanding key events are often at the heart of why someone works with a coach. Abraham Maslow (1943) is well known for his work on the hierarchy of human needs. In his work on *A Theory of Human Motivation*, he asserts that we move from being motivated by the most basic of needs to stay alive to the most transformative of human aspirations. His trajectory takes motivation along this continuum:

Physiological Safety → Love → Esteem → Self-Actualization.

This chapter is about self-actualization. Human behavior is motivated by the desire to improve the quality of life, and that means achieving the progressive satisfaction of the needs identified in Maslow's hierarchy. It's never a perfect process. The ability to work with the ups and downs of the journey and stay focused on the balance of embracing today while being hopeful about tomorrow is the crux of the challenge to authentically experience satisfaction. If he told the truth, we suspect Mick Jagger would have to admit he got a lot of joy throughout his career complaining about how he "can't get no satisfaction!"

We live in a world inundated with advertising. All those ads let us know in no uncertain terms that we aren't okay! We need better deodorant, hair color, shoes, clothes, homes, cars, whatever. All that constant advertising can create a blitz of internal messages based in self-doubt and inadequacy. This is why the people who are really adept at experiencing the joy of authentic success intentionally limit the amount of advertising they see or hear. It doesn't just mean they pay strict attention to the amount and type of radio and television they listen to and monitor which newspapers and magazines or journals they read. They're too busy being out in the rush of life trying and failing and succeeding and suffering and having fun to subject themselves to all that vicarious media.

To help your clients challenge the impact of the perfection trap in their lives, guide them to be realistic, to truly identify and celebrate successes, and to embrace the journey. If they can become grateful for what each day offers, they are a long way toward living a high-quality life.

## SELF-TALK: THE DISCIPLINE THAT MAKES A DIFFERENCE

Self-talk rules perception. How we explain and justify our experience to ourselves is enormously influential to our well-being. We can only contemplate, enjoy, and learn from our experiences when we are in touch with what they really are. This cannot happen if we are confusing our experiences with our judgments or assessments of them. This is one of the primary reasons we need to develop the practice of sitting quietly. Silence focuses us on spiritual development or the personal practice of improving our resilience to stress. Learning to quiet one's mind is one of the most profound practices we can personally engage in, and help our clients value. It isn't easy, yet the rewards can be exponential. Our minds are going most of the time; there may not be much of value being processed, but thinking is what our minds do, and do, and do.

This is one of the reasons it is important to take responsibility for the amount of media exposure we experience. The consumer psychologists who design advertising are masters at revving up the engines of our desire and pointing us toward this or that product, and we can never achieve authentic success if we are motivated by inauthentic desires. From a spiritual perspective, all desire tends to objectify the "wholeness" that which can never be acquired, but only received.

Draw on any of these points about self-talk that will best support your client. One central self-talk challenge is the way in which your clients characterize themselves internally. Do your clients beat up on themselves, constantly finding fault? Or do they reach for the other extreme, never allowing a real challenge to trouble them? Leaders in cognitive therapy have developed practical solutions that coaches can borrow. David Burns' book, *Feeling Good: The New Mood Therapy* (1980) is a classic in the field. It is full of concrete examples to use to turn negative thought patterns around to more supportive self-talk.

There can be a painful disparity between what your clients think "ought" to happen and what actually happens. Working with them to both clarify and challenge their "should" detector will influence their personal freedom and their ability to embrace a realistic interpretation of authentic success.


## HOW MUCH DO YOU ASK OF LIFE?

There's a poignant scene in the 2007 movie *Evening* starring several great actresses, including Vanessa Redgrave and Meryl Streep. Redgrave's character, Ann Lord, is an elderly woman about to die. Her college friend, Lila, has called to say goodbye. Streep plays Lila Ross, a well-to-do woman who settled for an appropriate marriage, while her friend Ann worked to become a singer in New York. Both had loved a young man named Harris, but neither married him. Raising concern that at least one of them should have married him, Ann is assured by Lila that it all worked out as it was supposed to be. The implication is that ultimately there are no mistakes. Yet Lila also observes that Ann had gone after so much in life, much more than Lila allowed herself to. She notes that there are big differences in how much people want from life and that that, too, is quite okay.

As Streep's character is leaving, Redgrave's daughter in the film asks for more information about her mom's life and Lila wisely says, "We are mysterious creatures, aren't we? Your mother had a whole life and none of us can know all about it."

These observations are interesting and provide tips to help your coaching clients achieve authentic success. Yes, of course your clients will want different levels of engagement out of life. They must be aware of their own drives and values to determine what is a blessing for them personally— glorious success for one could be pain and obligation for another. Your clients have the opportunity to live whole and mysterious lives, but it doesn't happen by accident. Rather, it happens when they pay attention to what matters for them and invest in that recognition with some passion to bring those preferences to light in their lives. It requires the willingness to make mistakes, forgive, and be grateful. All of these capacities relate to their emotional and social effectiveness.

## EI SKILLS SUPPORTING AUTHENTIC SUCCESS

As we're talking about a life well-lived with passion and focus, it's easy to line up every ESE strategy and its underlying EI skills as relevant to authentic success. Some of the most important include happiness, optimism, resilience, gratitude/forgiveness, resilience, self-regard, and self-discipline—all of these are contributors to self-actualization.

The ability to assist clients in growing their emotional and social intelligence is one of the best gifts a coach can bring to the coaching relationship. Research continues to validate that a positive ROI (return on investment) results when organizations strengthen relationships by working with these targeted behavioral areas, as discussed in Chapter Two on the business case. These are all can-do skills. If your clients want to enjoy authentic success, it is likely they will have to take risks, work hard, and engage with a great coach to help them break old patterns that feed today's misery or challenges. A few of the most important skills you may assist your clients with to expand their authentic success are highlighted below.

## Happiness

Goldie Hawn has one of the best smiles and most infectious laughs in the universe. She has a gift and no doubt lots of serotonin to support her positive, giggly persona. Emotions are contagious. Many of us grew up hearing the popular sentiment "Smile and the world smiles with you." Now science has shown that's not just folk wisdom, it's scientifically true (Barsade, 2002). So when we share our happiness, we make a world of difference. Goldie Hawn is one of a kind, but perhaps by following her example your clients can find their own unique ways to communicate their happiness. In the chorus of the Ninth Symphony, Beethoven quotes Schiller's instructions to "share thy joy and spend it freely!" We believe it's everyone's birthright to access that happiness, but how many of us ever make that discovery? Skillful coaching focuses on opening and engaging the emotional energy that connects your clients to the world and to each other. Helping your clients speak their truths and discern that truth from their opinions and assessments about how things should be, rather than seeking quick cognitive fixes, can be one of the best possible strategies for assisting people to know and extend this deep satisfaction. In other words, if Tomás doesn't get a promotion he seeks, he must objectively evaluate the situation: What did he do to contribute to the decision? Did he do his best at the interview? Does he really want the new position? Is he willing to apply again next time it opens? This line of questioning will help him grow from the difficult experience. On the other hand, he could choose to just rationalize the result with an "Ah, they don't like me anyway." In that line of responding, Tomas is likely to gain little.

The pursuit of happiness is a cherished ritual for all humans. That pursuit may feel rewarding if your clients are consciously focused and centered, or like hell if they have no idea what they are running after. The Dali Lama says happiness is one of the most universally sought of all human goals. The United States Constitution declares this right to be one that is given by God. Happiness isn't an accident, and it's not dependent on winning the lottery. True happiness includes embracing your whole self—the good, the bad, and the ugly. It is based on accepting the light and joyful moments as well as the dark moments. It is tied closely with the ESE competency of valuing self. It's intentional, and a good coach can help make an enormous difference in a client's ability to experience true happiness.

One of the best sources on this topic is Martin Seligman's *Authentic Happiness* (2002). He defines the key constituents of happiness as positive emotions and strengths. Seligman defines three types of happiness, beginning with the *pleasant life* that comes from physical pleasures, such as good food, flowers, and certainly chocolate. These hedonistic pleasures are always temporary. The second level is the *good life*, and that happens when you use your core strengths every day to produce an enduring sense of authenticity. As Seligman says, people experiencing the good life have an abundant sense of gratification. It affects all parts of life—work, love, and family. The third level is the *purposeful life*, which occurs when we know we're leading a meaningful life that goes beyond the personal gratification of the good life. Finding meaning entails connecting to something larger than develops in the good life. People find different ways to make this commitment. For some it is with social groups; for others environmental causes are their calling. Many take it to a spiritual level and discover a joy and grace that can support them through all of life's vicissitudes.

If your client complains about "just not being happy," there is a lot to unpack from this statement. It creates a beginning impression and that's all. Be sure you don't try to jump in and help your clients relieve their discomfort too soon. What they are experiencing is beginning to reveal to them their worldview and its consequences; the inquiry and exploration of this perception is the central work of coaching.

## Optimism

Logically inconsistent speaking patterns can be a saving grace. "How?" you might say? Well, it's true. If you speak of "good" things as if they are simply the norm, most likely to happen throughout your life, and "bad" things as if they are a most unusual bump in the road, your optimistic self-talk will promote a positive and resilient outlook on life. Better things are likely to happen for you, and your positive energy and positive outlook are likely to be reciprocated. Remember, emotions are contagious.

Seligman is also author of *Learned Optimism* (1991). As a founder of the field of positive psychology and well-known educator, he has been influential in provoking people to access their integrity and passion for life. He identified three categories of language patterns that affect optimism—permanence, pervasiveness, and personalization. The first two, permanence and pervasiveness, have to do with the length and depth of an impact or an event. If it's something you want to continue, an optimistic response will make it more likely. "I won 50 bucks playing lotto because great things always happen to me!" Rather than "I won 50 bucks playing lotto; that's totally weird! I'm never lucky." The third part calls for finding the balance between accepting responsibility for what happens in your life without overdoing it. An optimistic response is "I'm working closely with my supervisor to be sure I get a good assignment from her." A pessimistic response is "Even if I work with my supervisor, I'll probably get a lousy assignment. She just doesn't like me."

We know that when pessimistic people run into obstacles, they are likely to quit. When optimistic people are faced with the same obstacle, they'll feel more resourceful and probably start with the question of "How else can I accomplish this task?" Or they realize it's time to harness their patience if they want their efforts to pay off in the long run. Optimism + flexibility + curiosity = resilience! Take these ideas to your coaching practice and you will promote optimism through in building the awareness of how to use effective language patterns.

## SELF-ACTUALIZATION

*That only which we have within, can we see without.*
*If we meet no Gods, it is because we harbor none. If there is a*
*grandeur in you, you will find grandeur in porters and sweeps.*

RALPH WALDO EMERSON

Self-actualization is one of the most important EI skills. It's a measure of your sense that you have a meaningful personal engagement in life and that you are giving the gifts to your world that are most important for you to contribute. It's directly connected to motivation. If we are enthused by what we're doing, we're much more likely to approach it with zest. Reuven Bar-On (2001) wrote an excellent article on emotional intelligence and self-actualization that illustrates the intimate connection between the two. His research led him to conclude that "you can actualize your potential capacity for personal growth only after you are socially and emotionally effective in meeting your needs and dealing with life in general" (p. 85). His next words demonstrate that this is where coaches aim when we are participating in our clients' transformative growth. Bar-On said, "While emotional intelligence relates to being effective, self-actualization relates to doing the best you can possibly do. Or put another way, when we are self-actualized, we have gone beyond EI to achieve a higher level of human effectiveness."

We quoted Emerson at the beginning of this section because moving to this larger level of effectiveness means connecting with something larger than your individual self. Your coaching clients may often bring up religion or spirituality in the conversation. For many, this is home base, from which they develop trust, purpose, and values so it cannot be left out if you are to have a full conversation.

Other key dynamics for you to address when building self-actualization include your client's self-talk, self-assessment, and use of his or her strengths. How your clients view themselves is at the fulcrum of whether they're living in a world in which real growth is possible or one in which they likely feel hopeless that anything will ever get better. Your clients will make internal assessments of their capabilities, their purpose, and their value or worth. Many painfully short-change themselves; others may engage in grandiose thoughts. Those assessments then lead to self-talk, which is so important that we discussed it earlier in this chapter and gave you strategies for helping clients improve it. The talking machines in our heads go non-stop until we learn to control them, so it's important to manage the messages that tend to spill forth.

Research and common sense both tell us your clients will do better when they operate from their strengths. Those are gifts that they do well naturally and that engage their interest. When your clients focus on living from their strengths, much of the struggle can dissipate, freeing energy for growth. It's an extremely high probability that someone can only develop a sense of self-actualization by consistently engaging life from his or her strengths.

# LIFE'S 2% SOLUTION

Marcia's book, *Life's 2% Solution* (2006), provides a carefully developed ten-step plan for finding a viable path to personal fulfillment. Viable is a key word. Based on her research, she found that if busy professionals would dedicate 2 percent of their time—thirty minutes a day or three and a half hours a week—to doing something their hearts deeply call them to do, that their lives will work much better. The daily thirty minutes is critical. The only reason such a small amount of time works is because it is a consistent commitment, it is time spent with intention and focus, and it's engaging with something truly important to that person.

The process needs to include reflective time as well. We need to notice how we feel and why, notice what is gratifying and what chafes, and recognize the difference. Chafing is sometimes a necessary part of a growth process, but it's much more valuable if we consciously engage with it. If you work with this strategy, your clients will choose different 2 percent projects in different time spans of their lives. If your clients are in their twenties they may choose sports, people in their thirties are often developing a home or beginning a spiritual practice, and people in their sixties are likely to be focused on a hobby or volunteering as they have new amounts of free time. A 2 percent project might be poetry, pottery, or improving your putting in golf. What matters is that it's fulfilling to the individual. One effective way to work with your clients in developing their self-actualization, happiness, and optimism can be to use the structure of the 2% Solution.

When your clients recognize and live in accordance with their well-thought-through definitions of authentic success, they develop peace of mind. Don't get us wrong. We understand that life on planet earth is filled with messy and challenging circumstances. The invitation is to greet those circumstances with a sense of equilibrium. Living with passionate equilibrium is at the heart of one's 2% Solution. This unique notion captures our need for both zest and rest. It calls on us to recognize and embrace what we care about and to engage with it passionately, but not to spend so much energy that we lose our health, our families, or other treasures.

This balance is a result of lifelong intention to integrate the four domains of daily living—body, heart, mind, and soul. At times in your clients' lives, any one of these will capture more of their time and attention. It's not a requirement that they live by balancing exact amounts of time in each field, but it is important that they pay attention across the four domains. This means you help them ensure that they are aware of their bodies and honor them with exercise, nutrition, and rest. They remain aware of their hearts and honor them with loving relationships, listening to their higher calling, engaging others with compassion, and having fun. Your job as a coach is to help them stay aware of their cognitive health and nurture their minds with thoughts, challenging discussions, even good reading, and perhaps puzzles or chess. You help them engage or expand their awareness of their souls, or whatever term they use to characterize that which is bigger than they are. This circle of awareness and investment pays off. As they add healthy doses of gratitude, they will begin to savor more and more deeply the peace and joy and power of living authentic success.

## CHRISTA'S JOURNEY—COACHING FOR AUTHENTIC SUCCESS

*Christa:* Hey, Coach, What's up?

*Coach:* Good to see you, Christa. We had a big session last time. How are you?

*Christa:* Pretty good, well . . . actually, to use one of the emotionally descriptive words we've been talking about, I'm pensive because I'm really wrestling with this job change.

*Coach:* Great clarity, pensive tells me a lot! Tell me more.

*Christa:* Well, I do and don't want to take the offer at the new office. I love my current job. It's great being a part of corporate headquarters; there's a buzz here that doesn't happen anywhere else, and I know the job well. I have a great relationship with the CEO and in my next position I'd report to the regional director, so much of my connection to the top would be curtailed. What do you think I should do?

*Coach:* Sometimes it's tempting to get others to advise you on what you should decide, but you know you're the decision-maker here. Let's look at the list of concerns you raised and how it compares with the list of your core values and your strengths you developed in our last session.

*Christa:* Great! This sounds like we're putting a puzzle together and I love those kinds of challenges.

*Coach:* Okay, but don't get excited and rush by what you're noticing, and feeling, and questioning as we talk about these aspects.

*Christa:* Okay, my values: First, to really give all my gifts at work, I'm great at my job and love all the people connections I have. That's what gets me out of bed feeling gung ho about work. Second, I want to be respected at work. Charles, the CEO, does respect me and that's felt good, but there is a rub. Lately the new finance director gets the boss's ear so much that I don't get the quality time I used to. They're big buddies, golf together and all that. I'm worried I may be shut out even more. And third, I want to do good ethical work. That unquestionably happens, although I felt a real twinge last week when the finance director told me to cut down my number of client contacts to save money on the sample products we distribute. That will hurt sales, I'm sure of it.

*Coach:* Good, you've reviewed some of your values that we've talked about so far, but I haven't heard how they factor in at the new position. Also, as I've thought about our discussion, I keep wondering about you personally. There's a lot here about your work. What about you?

*Christa:* When I'm not at work, I'm tired. Driving forty miles each way in rush hour traffic to my current job is exhausting; often I just stay at work late to miss the traffic going home. Either way I get home too late to do much. I've really wanted to take up tennis again, but I just can't. I want to exercise more, and tennis is a love, but it just isn't practical. I take care of my house, mow the lawn, things like that. I don't have time for more. I don't know my neighbors or my community; I really live at work and then take vacations.

*Coach:* So work is a big part of your life, vacations happen, but you have little time at home and no time for the exercise you would really like to get going.

*Christa:* That's about it. My career rules. Yet, even as I say that my stomach tightens. It doesn't feel right. I used to love variety and new challenges. It's possible I'm stuck in a rut. But I do love my job! So why would I consider changing?

*Coach:* I have no idea, but it seems that you are. What would be satisfied if you did change? What else is important to you?

*Christa:* Well I miss home life; I usually just accept the current situation. Quite frankly I'd just accepted this as a part of the tradeoff for my great career. However, now that I'm aware of an option, different feelings are sneaking back in.

*Coach:* And what might those sneaky feelings be? What do they suggest you consider?

*Christa:* Well, in truth, I'm not as happy as I once was. I'm realizing my job is somewhat compromised by the power of the finance director, I'm tired from the drive and hungry for variety, and my job hasn't changed much for a long time. But I don't want to give you the wrong idea, I love my job.

*Coach:* You want to emphasize that you love your job, and at the same time, other feelings are giving you new considerations. What would happen if you responded to those new feelings?

*Christa:* It's scary, that's the other new feeling I haven't talked about. How could I be at the top of my game and all of a sudden not there any more? Would this change be a demotion? If I were to tell the truth, I feel like I've been demoted in place now that this new person is gaining so much power. Geez, this is too much!

*Coach:* It feels like a lot to you right now, doesn't it. It's scary and unsettling that your job has changed like this. How do those feelings fit in with those sneaky ones of not being as happy as you used to be and being tired of the commute? And why is it they seem to need to sneak?

*Christa:* Well [she takes a deep breath and sits quietly].

*Coach:* [Waits patiently.]

*Christa:* Hmm, did I tell you the new position is five miles from my house, can you believe that? It'd be a big challenge because it's opening a whole new sector of our business, and that's exciting. It's a bit scary, but in a positive way. I love challenges and it's been a long time since I've been challenged. There really are some good opportunities in the new position. I was so focused on my current job, I hadn't taken time to notice, but I actually have a vague sense of relief and happiness when I think of the new job. Wow, this is surprising information to me! Maybe I should just make the change right now!

*Coach:* [With a chuckle] You do love to be passionate about whatever you're engaged with and that's great. Did you tell me you have some time on this decision? [Helping her slow down and really experience the decision so she can feel comfortable with the process as well as the decision.]

*Christa:* Well, yes, I have two weeks before I need to decide. But I like being decisive, hanging out in uncertain land isn't my cup of tea!

*Coach:* How long have you been in your current job?

*Christa:* Ten years and I expect the same in the next one, maybe more.

*Coach:* For that amount of time, how about building in some personal reflecting time for you first. Take advantage of those two weeks and really live with your thoughts and feelings. Consider possibilities.

*Christa:* Ugh. I could do that, though it's not my style. You're right I have a lot at stake, but. . . .

*Coach:* [Stays silent.]

*Christa:* Well, it's hard to imagine a more important decision in my life. So I'd better invest in me, as you put it. Do you have any ideas on how to go about it?

*Coach:* Yes, you know how valuable I believe reflecting time is. That's taking time to think it through. You've started doing some journal writing. How about writing about the two jobs? First write in the present tense as if you already have chosen one—write what's great and not so great about that job and write about how you feel now that you don't have the other job. Then reverse the two jobs and repeat the process. See what comes up for you, and we'll talk about it in our conversation next week. Also, it would also be good to really talk in depth about this with a trusted friend or colleague who doesn't work for your company.

*Christa:* Well, I'll do the writing. And I miss my friend Caroline. She's a great businesswoman. I'll call her and set up a time, I think she's going through some changes in her life that will be good to catch up on as well.

*Coach:* That sounds great. Bring in the information next time and we'll explore further. I'm glad you're going to take time for yourself to fully consider this decision. Remember to consider your list of values as you do your writing. See which ones come to light the best or differently in the two jobs.

*Christa:* I'll do it. See you next week.

To experience the results of our lives as authentically successful, and in which we make meaningful contributions, the actions we take must arise from an emotional capacity that is free, open, and spontaneously engaging our world and the people in it. We have reviewed strategies for building this capacity, including understanding that is a lifelong journey that builds on the exercise of the first four ESE strategies. We listed first steps in clarifying your clients' definitions of success and their values. We also emphasized that this comprehensive strategy is built on the use of many skills, such as your clients' happiness and optimism, all of which contribute to their sense of living lives intentionally aimed at experiencing authentic success.

# PART THREE

# Developing the Coach

## By Guest Authors Julio Olalla and Terrie Lupberger

Coaching is fundamentally about learning—learning to take new actions, to behave differently, to see and engage in life more consistently with what matters most to you. In these two chapters we present key learning elements for good coaches in general and, more specifically, key elements for increasing your emotional competency and capacity as a coach.

Chapter Eight presents Newfield's Ontological Coaching™ approach, which is a different kind of conversation that aims to recover all territories of being human as domains of learning. It includes effective action and also transcends it to aim for effective living. Ontological coaching increases your possibilities for action by changing the observer you are. It alters your ability to act by producing awareness of emotional, cultural, social, and somatic aspects of your performance. It increases your capacity for action by changing the place you act from.

This chapter presents three doorways that Newfield coaches are trained to explore: (1) your client's use of language, (2) your client's bodily (somatic) shape and stance, and (3) your client's emotional awareness. These forms of learning all support coaching conversations that build emotional and social effectiveness.

In Chapter Nine we present four areas of learning for the coach that, if practiced with rigor and wholeheartedness, will increase your own emotional awareness and make you a more masterful coach in working with your clients. Those four areas are (1) Taking a look at the way you see and construct your reality, (2) learning to learn, (3) emotional immersion, and (4) practicing gentle irreverence.

# CHAPTER 8

# Emotions as a New Field of Learning

## *By Guest Authors Julio A. Olalla and Terrie Lupberger*

The Newfield Network, Inc., an international learning and coaching company, has been teaching coaching and leadership programs for almost two decades. At the core of our work is a newly emerging understanding of emotions, one that perceives emotions as an essential, generative force in creating the lives we want to live and the meaning that guides our actions, one that considers emotions as fertile territory for learning.

In this chapter we present a unique framework for coaching that will expand not only your understanding of coaching, but also your understanding of emotions as a powerful and non-discretionary force in generating sustainable change. Within this understanding, we discuss emotions as legitimate territories for learning that the coach can explore with clients to help them reshape their reality, actions, results, and future.

In this chapter we also distinguish three different pathways you, the coach, can travel with your client to support him or her in exploring new behaviors consistent with desired goals and outcomes. These pathways are interrelated and directly connected to your client's capacity for emotional awareness and intelligence.

Our aim here is to present you with a more expanded view of coaching and give you new concepts and ideas to try on in your coaching so you can better serve your clients.

## A HOLISTIC APPROACH TO COACHING

Typically, what is found in the mainstream practice of coaching is what we would call a *transactional* approach and methodology. This means, as a client, if you do not like the results you are getting, your coach would work with you to identify new actions you need to take in order to produce your objectives. For example, John, the client, hires a coach to learn how to speak better in front of groups. A purely transactional approach would be for the coach to identify what action steps John could take, such as reading related books and articles, attending speaking classes, or joining the National Speakers Association or Toastmasters. The coach would ask John for dates by when John would commit to take each action step. During the coaching conversations, the coach would check in with John to see whether the action steps were taken, discuss why or why not, and likely get a new commitment to action if John didn't follow through.

While this way of working with a client can be very useful, we believe it is insufficient. A transactional approach to coaching doesn't challenge the clients' way of seeing. It doesn't have them question how their way of seeing and doing things might be limiting what is possible or getting in the way of what they want. It doesn't help clients understand how their emotional competencies are impacting their situations or how to increase their emotional responses for more effective outcomes.

In a transformational approach to the previous example, the coach might explore what motivates John to want to be a better speaker. John says it's because his team isn't responding to him as well as he wants. He goes on to say that if he were a better communicator, he could connect better with them and inspire them more powerfully. Now the coach can probe even further and ask what "connecting" would look like. How would he know? What would be different in the actions of his team? Does his team share these opinions of him? Would they say this is his leadership challenge or would they say he is looking in the wrong place? By exploring the way John sees and articulates his concern that brought him to coaching in the first place, the coach and client have richer possibilities for getting to the underlying issues and addressing the real concerns that are often hidden from us as we go about daily life. Through the process John could even draw on several of the emotional strategies, beginning with Responsive Awareness, to support him in achieving his desired outcomes.

Here's a classic example of when transactional coaching doesn't go far enough. The coach is working with a client; let's call her Mae, who has a habit of saying yes to the requests of others when she wants to say No. Never saying No to the requests of others is a foolproof recipe for overwhelm. Mae *Knows* she needs to say No and yet she doesn't do so when asked for help. She even practices with her coach on ways to say No that feel genuine and authentic, and yet she still says Yes. Knowing, in this example (and even the actions of practicing with her coach), are still insufficient to create the new future she wants. Mae's coach needed to have a different kind of conversation to support her in building her emotional awareness and the competence to say No. The coach might explore what saying No means to Mae. The coach could explore Mae's fears of not fulfilling everyone else's expectations of her. The coach might help Mae build the emotional capacity of courage so that, in the face of her fear, she could still take the action and also accept the consequences of her actions. The coach could work with Mae to help her develop the stance and bodily posture for saying No—and develop the capacity to stand in the face of anger or rejection if the person receiving the no goes to those emotional places as a reaction.

We certainly agree that new actions often are necessary to generate a different outcome. Our point is that after training thousands of coaches over the last two decades in many countries, and also assessing the coaching competencies of hundreds and hundreds of coaches, we continually see the tendency for coaches to rush to get their clients into new actions and new solutions without having the clients also question or examine the way they are seeing or explaining their reality as it impacts those actions.

An excerpt from a recently observed coaching session between a coach in training and his client illustrates the problem of not noticing and responding to emotional information:

*Client:* I'm a pretty competent business person, and yet my general contractor and I aren't even speaking to each other right now. I just want a schedule from him as to when his company will be done with the renovation. He is always late. I'm so frustrated and mad at him. The funny part is that I seem to turn into a babbling idiot when I go to speak with him.

*Coach:* So let's practice having a conversation with him. Does that seem like a good place to start?

*Client:* Okay.

*Coach:* Pretend I'm your contractor and say to me what you want to say right now.

*Client:* Ugh, well . . . let's see. . . . John, you've been working on my house for two months and you're running behind schedule and you keep making promises to me that you don't follow through on. I'm really frustrated and I'd like a schedule from you that you are going to keep.

*Coach:* Great. How did that feel?

*Client:* Pretty good.

*Coach:* Do you think you could say that to John?

*Client:* Yes, I think so.

*Coach:* Do you need to write it down?

*Client:* No, I can remember that.

*Coach:* So, by when will you have this conversation with John?

*Client:* I can do it next time we meet, which I think is . . . next Thursday.

We wish we could say this session went on to a brilliant end and that the coach asked the client questions that helped her get to underlying issues. The coach rushed right to taking care of the issue that the client first presented (a mostly ineffective move in coaching) and produced very little by the end of the conversation. The coach missed the opportunity to have the client take a look at the emotions she was caught in and triggered by. The coach could have explored with the client whether this situation felt familiar to her in any other areas of her life. There was no inquiry as to the client's responsibility for the relationship becoming so difficult. There was no conversation about building the client's emotional strategies for navigating what she considered to be a difficult conversation. There could have been a conversation about whether she was avoiding valuing herself or the contractor because of her emotional skill level. This coaching was superficial at best and the client was not served by this coach, who was caught in a solution-oriented, problem-solving trap of coaching.

## NEWFIELD'S ONTOLOGICAL COACHING™ APPROACH

Newfield's coaching methodology provides for a different kind of conversation that powerfully integrates both the transactional and transformational approaches. We call it Ontological Coaching™ and it is a process by which the coach supports the client in recognizing and revising the habitual thinking, ways of being and acting that are in the way of generating sustainable new behaviors and actions. Newfield's Ontological Coaching approach aims for effective action while also aiming for effective living. In Ontological Coaching, clients are supported in having conversations in which they *can* see new paths of thinking and actions to take that are consistent with what they most care about. *Yes!* The clients do practice new behaviors and actions. At the same time, the conversations, held in a respectful and non-judgmental emotional context by the coach, allow for sincere reflection and the building of new cognitive and emotional practices to replace ineffectual habits and generate more satisfaction. This coaching methodology increases the clients' capacity for action by changing the guiding thoughts and behaviors from which they act and make decisions on how to act. This promotes the ability to build emotional and social effectiveness.

When you as a coach assist your clients in building new awareness *plus* powerful practices, over time, your clients will generate greater effectiveness in action and sustainable well-being. Newfield Network founder, Julio Olalla in *From Knowledge to Wisdom* (2004a, p. 7) wrote:

> I am convinced that Ontological Coaching™ is one of the most effective methodologies for transformation available today—both personal transformation and organizational transformation.

The word "ontology" itself is foreign to most. Simply put, it is the branch of philosophy dealing with being in general and its properties. It is also defined as 'any particular theory of reality.' Ontological coaching addresses the concern for more effective action while also addressing the concerns of the human soul that are mostly left out of our learning practices today.

This is important to you, the coach, because addressing the whole human being, both the desire for better results and increased well-being, should be the aim of good coaching. For a myriad of historical and cultural reasons that are addressed in depth in Julio Olalla's book, *From Knowledge to Wisdom*, we as Western culture have over-emphasized and over-privileged the importance of achievement and results at the cost of well-being, meaning, and satisfaction, all components of emotional intelligence. We believe that coaching emerged as a profession at this time on the planet to re-integrate meaning with action and results for the sake of a healthier self and a healthier planet.

## EMOTIONS AND LEARNING

One of the fundamental tenets of Newfield's coaching approach, and the subject of this book, is that new emotional competencies can be learned and practiced for the sake of living more meaning-filled and successful lives.

Traditionally, learning itself has been viewed as the acquisition, manipulation, consumption, accumulation, and utilization of information. Learning has come to be about gathering and applying information to produce ever more objective, quantified results. Is it any wonder, then, that our children are turned off by school, seeing it as more or less irrelevant to their more spontaneous experience of daily living? Or why the executives running an organization can't understand how it is that employees aren't passionately engaged in the mission?

Where is the learning that addresses our capacity to relate with and engage others in a shared future? Where is the learning that encourages us to self-reflect? That teaches us optimism, self-regard, empathy, and compassion? That teaches us courage, how to value others, and how to value ourselves appropriately? That allows us time and processes to reflect on the nature and scope of the human condition and arrive at new solutions to face the current complexities of life as required if we are to live with authentic success?

A different, perhaps less common view of learning, and one that coaches must embrace, is that learning allows you to expand the way you see and take action in your life. Learning allows you to "do" something different, certainly, but learning also allows you to "see" differently, to expand your understanding and your world views, to examine the assumptions and beliefs from which you habitually take action, and maybe most importantly, to enhance the way you engage and relate with others. This view of learning requires us to embrace the critical importance of including emotions as a legitimate aspect of its territory.

Imagine, for a moment, that your client has been asked to lead a new team in the development of a software application for her company. She is resentful of this change and unaccepting of the circumstances. Now imagine you work with her to learn to approach this change with the emotion of joy. Which emotion will serve her best in this new assignment? In which emotion will the goals of the team be most effectively achieved? In resentment she is more likely to blame others and search for agreement that the change isn't good. In the emotion of joy, she is likely to be more inclined to believe in a positive future, and the outcomes of her conversations will be very different with herself and with others than if she is resentful. Which emotion will have the most positive impact on the bottom line? Unfortunately for their employees and shareholders, many organizations still consider emotional learning and emotional intelligence as merely the soft (and less important) side of HR, but this kind of learning has a direct impact on the bottom line.

In this overly simplified example, you can see that the emotional context from which we act (*and talking and thinking IS action*) generates what is possible in the future. As a coach, it becomes imperative to learn to understand, distinguish, and expand the emotions that influence your clients' actions on an everyday basis and in all domains of life. This will certainly give your clients a better chance of generating the outcomes they seek.

Applying this specifically to organizational life, the goal of the executive coach and of the leader coaching others is to facilitate the generation of the right emotional context to support the actions consistent with the goals/aims/desired outcomes of that individual or organization. A cool head, neutrality, or emotion-less clarity, are no longer the holy grails sought in leadership. You've heard that old saying that "the right words, in the wrong emotion, are the wrong thing to say."

## THREE POWERFUL DOORWAYS IN COACHING

Another of Newfield's fundamental tenets is that, as human beings, our reality or worldview is shaped by many things. The stories we have been told by history, family, culture; the assumptions, largely untested, that we live our life by; the way we explain reality; the beliefs and values we hold; the way we use language; the emotions we habitually fall into blindly; the way we physically stand and move, the systems in which we live and work—all these elements go into forming the way we see the world and thus interact with it and create results. As a coach, you have all these pathways or doorways as possibilities to explore when supporting your clients to get into new actions to reach their declared goals.

Three powerful doorways that Newfield coaches are trained to explore are: (1) your clients' use of language—meaning the conversations they are able to have and the ones they are not able to have, the way they make requests or offers, the way they explain their circumstances or tell their stories; (2) your clients' bodily (somatic) shape and stance—meaning how they physically present themselves in action and what their presence generates in others; and (3) your clients' emotional awareness—meaning their capacity to invoke the appropriate emotional responses for their circumstances and desired outcomes. (Since this book is on the topic of emotional intelligence, this doorway is the focus of our attention, but the other two are briefly explained a little further in this chapter.)

Of course these doorways aren't the only ones! The social systems we are born into, the era and epoch we are living in now, our relationship to the cosmos, our religious or spiritual beliefs . . . all impact the world we see and thus the actions we take. As a professionally trained coach, it is your responsibility to be aware of the myriad of influences that limit your and your clients' capacity for actions. Your work as a professional coach is to assist your clients in challenging the emotional as well as the cognitive and somatic habits they have developed over time that are keeping them from their goals and dreams and to support them in the learning they need to succeed.

Let's explore each of these three doorways in a little more depth so you can begin to use them in your own coaching.

## EMOTIONS AND LANGUAGE

From an evolutionary standpoint, emotions preceded language. The limbic system, where emotion originates, is thousands of years older than the neo-cortex, where rational thought and language exist. Simply put, we were emotional beings long before we had language. Lewis, Amini, and Lannon state in *A General Theory of Love* that "Emotions reach back one hundred million years, while cognition is a few hundred thousand years old at best. Despite their youth, the prominent capacities of the neocortical brain dazzled the Western world and eclipsed the mind's quieter limbic inhabitant. Because logic and deduction accomplish so plainly, they have been presumed the master keys that open all doors" (2000, p. 228).

We now know with great advances in brain research that the part of the brain where emotions live is a different part of the brain from where our reasoning lives, and these separate brains respond very differently—even to the same stimuli. A simple case in point, have you ever been to a work function such as a retirement party or awards ceremony and, prior to your attendance, you told yourself you were not going to cry. After all, the senior leaders will be present, and tearing up in front of them won't serve the leadership identity you are seeking to create for yourself. And . . . you cry anyhow . . . which points to the fact that the limbic system, the emotional "house" of the brain, doesn't respond to your linguistic commands. In fact, it could care less!

This is important to coaching because so many coaches rush to get their clients into new actions that ultimately fail. Taking new actions requires a new emotional space or stance to act from. Simply telling a client to stop getting triggered when the boss criticizes his or her work performance in front of others will not result in the client being less triggered. The emotional system doesn't respond to commands.

We were emotional beings long before humankind had the capacity for language. When human beings developed language, it then became the water we swam in to the point that only in the last century did we undertake to understand the impact that language itself has on our capacity for action. The fundamental assumptions we have lived with for thousands of years about human language have been that it is a code we share and use to describe how things are, out there—in reality. Language has been viewed as passive and fundamentally separated from action. Language was assumed to refer to action, but it wasn't considered action itself.

This perception began to change during the linguistic revolution that took place in philosophy at the beginning of the last century. The Oxford philosopher J.L. Austin began a critical revision of those assumptions, and through his work and those that followed him (including University of California professor of philosophy, John Searle), we now have come to realize that language not only *describes* "reality" or "experience" but it can also generate a new future or outcome. A simple example is Jennifer who, after being in her organization for two years, was lagging in performance for the first time in her career. The organizational structure had become more complex during that time, and she now had multiple customers to satisfy as opposed to the original two. Her wise manager asked Jennifer to interview all of her stakeholders and ask two questions: "What am I doing well?" and "What do you see I need to learn to improve my performance?" Jennifer resisted these conversations for weeks, coming back to her manager with the same story: "This is hard and I'm feeling very vulnerable. I don't want to be attacked." Noticing the habit in her language, Jennifer's manager coached her to change her story that these conversations would be hard. She had Jennifer create and practice a new story that having these kinds of conversations was an essential component of becoming an organizational leader and how they would support her in moving to the next level within the organization. Jennifer's new story created a new future for herself that wasn't available in the old story.

As human beings, we have largely been unaware that language is shaping the world we live in. When we take our car to the mechanic because it just doesn't run right, the mechanic listens to the engine, describes the noise as two metal spoons banging together, and then we are able to hear what we didn't hear before. We have a new distinction generated out of language that allows us to listen for that in the future and that allows the mechanic to intervene in a malfunction we didn't recognize before we learned that new distinction.

This happens all the time when we engage in conversations with people who share with us distinctions we did not have before. That, exactly, is the role of a coach and also of a leader. In working with Jerome, a senior leader at a retail chain, his coach had interviewed six of his stakeholders prior to beginning the coaching engagement. The stakeholders all reported, to varying degrees, that they felt manipulated (their exact words) by Jerome and as a result did not trust him. Jerome's coach was able to offer a powerful distinction to Jerome between manipulation and influence, the latter being an emotional capacity to enroll others into your way of seeing in which the other chooses that over a previously held way of seeing. Influencing is a very different move in leading than manipulation, which is forcing or tricking others down a path of action without their buy-in, consent, or enrollment—often through false or incomplete information. The coach then had Jerome pay attention in his conversations with the stakeholders and to notice each time he sensed he was manipulating rather than creating influence. This practice gave the coach and the client great conversational material to further identify old behaviors for Jerome to drop and new ones to put in place to rebuild trust. These are strategies that build his ESE competency in valuing others.

Our language is an essential element in constituting all of us as the unique observers we are, in creating the *me* who sees what I see and the *you* who sees what you see. Through the power language grants us to make distinctions, and by enabling us to make things happen, we are able to transform ourselves and the actions we take. That's the power you assist your clients in developing. One word to describe what you do as a coach is "story-buster." You listen carefully to the way your clients explain their situations. You listen carefully to the conversations they fall into and the ones they can't or don't seem to have. You point this out to them and explore with them new possibilities to replace the habits in language that aren't working.

Of course, this topic of how language shapes our reality could be the subject of an entire book in itself—and a good one to reference is *Language and the Pursuit of Happiness* by Chalmers Brothers (2004). In Ontological Coaching we distinguish five basic acts in speech that have enormous implications on the kind of results we produce or do not produce. The important point for this book is that you, the coach, begin to understand that the way your clients speak, the language they use and the stories they tell are not innocent. They shape what is possible.

Additionally, a separation of language from emotions is an artificial one. Language lives braided with emotions. Language is never isolated, never separated from the world of emotions. Every time you speak, you speak from your historical background of emotional habits and generate an emotional context in which you are listened to by others. There is no such thing as unemotional thinking or unemotional conversing. Your every internal and external conversation is already coming from a particular emotional space, as well as containing the built-in potential to impact and change the emotional state of others.

Another way to understand emotions is as predispositions for action, that is, they have the result of pre-disposing us toward certain actions and away from others. If I am angry, I will act in one way. If I am courageous, I will act in a different way. A critical role of the coach is to help reveal the consequences of the clients' conversations and the emotions the conversations are held within. The coach helps the client see his or her habits of speaking and emoting that interfere with generating desired outcomes. The coach offers the possibility of new learning and a new set of choices. It takes a strong process of reflection and well-designed practices to escape from our conversational inertia and habits and from their limiting consequences.

## EMOTIONS AND THE BODY

As we have just explored, your actions are shaped by your language as well as by your emotions. There is an inextricable interplay between these two.

There is also another critical element in Ontological Coaching™ that shapes how you see and take action. Just as your linguistic and emotional being has been ignored in our traditional understanding of learning, the domain of the body and biology has, in large part, been neglected as well. The concept of embodied learning is only recently making its way into the fringes of mainstream learning. The famous cognitive biologists, Humberto Maturana and Francisco Varela, wrote a magnificent book, *The Tree of Knowledge* (1987) on the subject of how our biology shapes our understanding of reality. Written in 1987, it was a radical departure from the current commonsense understanding. In it they wrote: "Indeed, we will propose a way of seeing cognition not as a representation of the world 'out there', but rather as an ongoing bringing forth of a world through the process of living itself" (p. 9).

This means that the act of discovering and knowing our world and environment is not just one of recognition, but a generative process that gives shape to our reality out of the form and process of our biology itself. Learning is not just a cognitive process. Learning happens in and through the body; it is a structural, biological transformation.

A more and more commonly heard phrase in the coaching profession that describes this phenomenon is called "somatic learning" or somatic coaching. Soma comes from the Greek language meaning: of or pertaining to the body.

Having competence in somatic coaching is critical in supporting your emotionally intelligent coaching because it suggests that learning new emotions generates a structural shift in your physiology and, correspondingly, new emotions can be generated and sustained through a shift in your physiology. As a coach, you can work with your clients' shape/body/physiology to help them generate and sustain a new emotional stance or competence.

For example, if your client is living in the predominant emotion of pessimism, her physiological structure will shape consistently with that emotion: she will tend to have drooping shoulders, a deflated chest, looser muscle tension, more shallow breathing, etc. If you want to help her generate a different emotion—say optimism—you can, of course, listen for her habits in language and work with her story that's keeping her stuck, as we described earlier. But you can also work with your client through this powerful doorway of body and help her reshape her physical stance to generate a different structure that actually allows for and encourages this new emotion. You might have her practice keeping her chest out and shoulders back when she is in a meeting, for example. You might have her practice deeper breathing, or give her simple martial art moves to elicit her warrior energy. The possibilities for working with our body and shape are endless.

In our Western, commonsense understanding of learning, we have little understanding of the close connection between our bodies and our emotional states, or with our bodies and the conversations we habitually fall into, but research has shown them to be highly coherent. Generally, we are unaware of the impact we have on others as a result of how we stand in the world or shape ourselves in conversations with them. We have little recognition that our physical and emotional health impacts our presence and our capacity to engage others in a common goal. While this is probably one of the oldest and paradoxically the newest territories of learning for us in the Western world, it makes sense that the power and influence we have with others is generated not only out of what we say, but out of the emotions and bodies we say it in.

Very often the biggest difficulty in learning something new is a body shaped against that possibility, a body that is rigid, tight, controlled. It is a profoundly important aspect of coaching or leading to be attuned to this constant pull toward coherence between our emotional being, our linguistic being, and our body.

Brandon was promoted to sales manager of a ten-person team about a year ago. His boss hired a coach for him because his team's sales goals were down 4 percent from the prior year. His boss liked Brandon and didn't want to fire him, plus Brandon had a technical understanding of the product that almost no one else on the sales team had. The coach hired to work with Brandon asked whether he could shadow Brandon for a month, including attending the weekly sales meetings that Brandon led.

At these meetings, the coach assessed that Brandon was tentative and distracted in his speaking and lacked the emotions of conviction, courage, and passion. Correspondingly, Brandon conducted these meetings sitting in a chair and in a posture that was slouched (his body was always positioned more down and back than up and forward). His eyes frequently looked down, and his voice would often be soft so that others had to strain to hear him.

Brandon's presence did not convey what Brandon intended nor what was needed to inspire the sales team. While there were many doorways the coach could have chosen to work in, he started by working with Brandon in the somatic territory. He first had Brandon become aware of how he typically sat, moved, and held himself in the sales meetings. The coach worked with Brandon on what his underlying concerns were for being in the manager role and what private thoughts and emotions (worry, hope, anxiety) he had about his abilities to do a good job in this role. He asked Brandon what his desired outcomes of the sales meetings would be, what emotions would support those outcomes, and also what presence would be needed from Brandon to invoke those emotions and outcomes. The coach then had

Brandon practice a different presence—a different physical stance—one that was consistent with what he wanted to achieve with his team. After four months, Brandon led the quarterly sales review with his team and boss in attendance. His boss publicly remarked at the end of the meeting that he was delighted at the new level of confidence Brandon exuded, and two of his team members publicly acknowledged being inspired and honored to work with Brandon as their leader.

If new emotions are to be learned, then, correspondingly, a new shape or body must be learned to hold the new emotion. Sustainable learning requires embodiment. Again, this is a powerful opportunity in coaching, but one to which most coaches are blind or are incompetent to handle. Our experience in coaching is that often a shift in the shape or body creates not only a shift in the emotion but in the story as well. Given how many senior leaders we coach, our experience proves time and time again that powerful leaps in leading come less from the coaching that offers new cognitive or intellectual insights and more from working with the client in the emotional and somatic territories.

## EMOTIONS, COACHING, AND MEANING

If the emotional place you take action from impacts what you produce, then the skill of generating powerful emotional contexts that support what you want to achieve becomes a critical coaching skill. One of the things that coaches do is connect people to what matters to them—with what gives them meaning.

Interestingly, meaning itself resides in an emotional space. Meaning is inconceivable without emotion; it is not an intellectual construction, but rather an emotional response to what matters to us. We can convey huge amounts of information and knowledge, but these cannot generate the sense of meaning that arises spontaneously in us parents, for example, when our child runs up and gives us a big hug. In that moment, we experience meaning and a sense of connectedness that simply cannot be reproduced any other way. One of the things that sets human beings apart from other species is our desire for—our craving for—meaning.

You may be familiar with the parable of the stone cutters. One day a man walking by a stone cutter asked him what he was doing. He replied: "I am breaking these stones into smaller ones and breaking my back in the process." The next day the man walked by a different stone cutter and asked him what he was doing. He replied: "I am building a cathedral." The stone cutters were taking the same actions but attributed very different meaning to their work and lived in very different emotional places.

Applied to organizational life, executive coaches support leaders in connecting people in the organization with a sense of purpose and meaning. One of the deepest challenges we consistently face in the organizational coaching work that Newfield does is finding how to help people deal with the sense of emptiness and meaninglessness that arises from their actions when they see them as disconnected from any overt sense of purpose or with what matters to them. That is why developing the ESE strategy of authentic success is so fundamental to coaching.

At its best, Newfield's ontological coaching approach is a multidisciplinary enriched practice of a new kind of learning, called into existence to re-integrate and address all the dimensions of being human—including our emotional lives—that, through an unchecked worship of science and rationalism, Western culture has dismissed or ignored over the last several hundred years. It isn't by lack of good will or intention that most coaching schools and most leadership programs are missing one of the most critical competencies in leading—generating the emotions and the emotional contexts needed to get the job done. They are, after all, caught in the same traditional and restrictive understanding and paradigm of learning we have referred to in this chapter. It is out of this very concern, desire, and belief in the power of emotions that we were called to contribute to this book.

In this chapter we have provided you with a brief introduction to Newfield's ontological coaching approach and have explored three essential territories when coaching others: language, emotions, and body. As a coach, on the path of mastery, you support your clients to learn—cognitively, emotionally, and somatically. You help your clients learn to have the conversations, emotional awareness, and somatic presence that will have the greatest impact and influence in accomplishing their desired outcomes. To ignore any of these dimensions in coaching means you are not addressing

A Coach's Guide to Emotional Intelligence

the whole person and you are leaving out rich and deep territory for more powerful learning.

And, as we have seen, these three territories are interwoven. To be an effective coach, you must develop your own conversational, emotional, and somatic competencies. The following chapter addresses further strategies for you, the coach, in building your own emotional competencies.

# CHAPTER 9

# Developing Your Own Emotional Awareness as a Coach

*By Guest Authors Julio Olalla and Terrie Lupberger*

**A** senior executive at a Fortune 1000 company recently said in a coaching session: "I'm basically at the top of my game professionally and yet I'm not enjoying being here. I don't find joy in my work anymore and the hours are insane, but the salary and accolades are hard to walk away from. What do I do?" This is a common statement among the executives we coach. Interestingly enough, it's not a question that can be answered with a traditional solution of "learn this skill set" or "acquire that information" and everything will be fine.

This kind of coaching exploration requires a coach who is competent at both the transformational and transactional approaches to coaching, as we discussed in the previous chapter.

It requires a coach who has developed his or her own emotional awareness so he or she has the competency and skills to guide the client through deep reflection of years of habits in thinking and acting to greater self-discoveries and awareness. It requires understanding of the ESE strategy of authentic success and that you are working on developing authentic success for yourself.

What brought the senior executive at that Fortune 1000 company to coaching wasn't a desire to learn to be more effective or efficient. What brought him to coaching was a desire to learn how to be satisfied with his accomplishments and generate authentic success. The goals he established for himself at the beginning of the coaching relationship were about redesigning a future with more meaning and passion. This meant he would need the courage to look at his automatic assumptions, habits, and responses, and it would require him to learn new emotional competencies.

This book has presented you with five strategies for emotional growth along with practices and examples that can benefit not only your clients, but you as well. We recommend that you take the Bar-On EQ-i® assessment and see how you score in the competencies highlighted, which are cross-referenced to these five strategies in Chapter One. You can then identify the areas you want to focus on in your emotional learning and design practices to support building your capacities in the five strategies of Valuing Self and Others, Responsive Awareness, Courage, and Authentic Success.

In addition to these, Newfield offers four additional strategies we will discuss in this chapter. More than strategies, these four represent enormous territories for personal growth and learning. Whether you are a beginning coach or a more experienced coach, these strategies can enhance your personal life as well as help you better coach your clients in developing their greater emotional awareness. In this chapter, we provide additional practical ideas for building your ESE capacity and in helping your clients develop their best ESE selves.

These four strategies are:

1. Take a look at how you take a look,
2. Learn how to learn,
3. Emotional immersion, and
4. The art of gentle irreverence.

Throughout this book we have emphasized that coaching is fundamentally about learning—learning to take new action and learning to think differently, which require new emotional capacities and awareness. Through the practice of coaching, you do facilitate learning information and knowledge, and you also facilitate learning new emotional moves, new emotional responses, and the new emotional receptivity the client needs to achieve his or her desired outcomes.

A critical question for you, the coach reading this book, should be emerging: How do I, as a coach, build my own emotionally responsive awareness so that I am more effective in my life and can also better serve my clients? In addition to the core ESE strategies already presented: Valuing Self and Others, Responsive Awareness, Courage, and Authentic Success, we offer the following ideas, stories, and practices to assist you in this question.

## 1. TAKE A LOOK AT HOW YOU TAKE A LOOK

As human beings, we all have a particular way of seeing and explaining the world around us and our place in it. The way we see our reality is shaped by myriad influences that are largely transparent to us, as we discussed in the previous chapter. One of the many gifts that coaching can be for others is a safe place to explore, examine, and even challenge the assumptions we base our thinking and actions on. While this is the territory of coaching, it is also an essential step in personal growth and development, since our automatic habits and assumptions are in the way of us getting what we desire.

So, how do you begin to examine the assumptions that inform your thinking? And how is that related to the actions you take or don't take? Here's a practice for you:

Carve out at least twenty minutes of time where you can be in a quiet and reflective space. Take out a notebook and write down what comes to you as you consider a few of these questions, specifically as each relates to your role as coach: What do you believe are the responsibilities of being a coach? What is coaching for you? Why does it matter to you, really? How do your answers serve your coaching, and how do they limit your coaching? What values do you hold as essential in life? How does that serve you as a coach? How does that not serve you in the role of coach? Do you believe human beings have a purpose or reason for being here? If so, what is that? And how does that serve and limit you in life and in coaching? What do you believe about human potential? How does what you believe serve you in your coaching and not serve you in your coaching?

What emotions do you feel are most essential to you being a great coach? Are you competent at these emotions? Take time to work with these questions and work with your own coach if that's possible.

The list of questions is endless, and you can come up with questions for every domain of life. For example, imagine you are a mom, and you want to explore the assumptions and beliefs you have about that and how they are serving or not serving you. What does being a mom mean to you? Why does it matter? What are your standards or conditions of satisfaction for being a mom? Are your actions consistent with those standards? Are those your standards or do some of them come from other sources (culture, tradition, spouse, family, etc.)? What is your predominant emotion in your role as mom? Does that serve you? If not, what do you need to learn?

This practice of taking a look at the assumptions you base your thinking and your actions on requires an enormous amount of courage and skill because you are examining and challenging the core assumptions and presuppositions that you live your life by and the habits of relating and taking action that result from those beliefs.

To demonstrate how an experienced coach applies this skill, let's look at an example of a coach working with his client, Erika, to help her take a look at how she's been taking a look so that she is empowered to take new action consistent with what she cares about.

Erika was a lobbyist for a national educational organization. Her boss asked her to find a coach because many in the organization had a negative assessment of her communication skills; they felt she was too abrupt and direct and often dismissive of others' ideas. When Erika met with her coach, she was very frustrated with the organization saying: "They want me to act differently than who I really am. What I do works. The lawmakers respect me and I produce miracles for this organization." Erika went on to say that her directness and abruptness was exactly what best served her in her lobbying role on Capitol Hill. She had never missed her goals, and the organization was very satisfied with the results she was producing among the lawmakers.

What Erika's coach helped her see through several coaching sessions was not that Erika needed to change "who she is." Rather, what Erika needed was a wider range of emotional moves that would lead to better conversations and relationships. The coach worked with Erika not to get rid of what was working, but to help her develop greater emotionally responsive awareness and sensitivity in her interpersonal relationships with the rest of her stakeholders so that she could meet them where they were, not where she was. Erika was asked to take a look at how she takes a look. Her coach asked her to examine some of the assumptions and beliefs she had about herself and about her role that might be getting in her way of reaching her goals.

Erika reported to her coach that her belief was that she had to be "tough," to put on a coat of armor every day she had to go to the Hill to lobby. Erika also mentioned to her coach that she was good at it and that her childhood memories were also of being "tough," as she was the only girl in a family of five older brothers. With further probing, Erika revealed to her coach that her husband often complained about her abruptness and insensitivity to his dreams and desires. These issues were explored in the coaching conversations and revealed to the coach and to Erika the linguistic, emotional, and somatic habits that Erika had developed for responding to many of life's situations. Erika's coach helped her practice building a wider repertoire of emotional responses and reactions to support her in creating more of what she wanted—better relationships at work and within her family.

The coach had Erika do the following three simple, but effective practices for developing greater emotional awareness.

1. Erika started asking her organizational colleagues how they were doing at every opportunity. Erika typically skipped over this aspect of relationship building and impulsively launched into what she wanted without noticing the cost of doing so. It was difficult at first; in fact Erika thought it was a waste of precious time when she first started her new practices, but she reported in the fourth month of the coaching relationship that she felt it had clearly changed her relationships with some of her key colleagues for the better. Her boss agreed, as she was receiving fewer complaints from colleagues these days about Erika's bad manners and temperament.

2. The coach worked with Erika to have her consciously slow down her pace when speaking with her colleagues. Initially this was very hard for Erika, but as we mentioned in the previous chapter, your emotional capacity is directly linked to your body—to the way you hold and shape your physical self. By physically slowing down her pace of conversations, she was able to be more emotionally present in her conversations.

3. Erika was challenged to ask at least 50 percent more questions in every conversation than the number of opinions she offered. Erika reported that she started doing this at home with her husband, who noted what a huge shift he saw in her as a result of the coaching.

The coach helped Erika take at look at how she takes a look, to re-examine her habitual ways of seeing and acting, and assess what she needed to learn in order to be more successful.

Questioning the worldviews that your clients have constructed and exploring how that impacts their capacity to design and execute a desired future is part of masterful coaching. It is an art because it requires right timing and the right mood to do it well. In our experience of coaching individuals and organizations all over the world, it does take time to build the trust and rapport needed to go into this territory, but once established, the learning and growth of the client is exponential and transformational.

As a coach, to first develop this skill for yourself, the best practice is to create the time and space on a regular basis to question your assumptions and beliefs in all domains of your life and to be courageous in challenging those that you see are getting in your way of what you want.

## 2. LEARN HOW TO LEARN

There are many areas in our lives in which we develop a certain resistance to learning and consequently go on performing actions that are ineffective.

Learning how to learn is a fundamental competence for a coach. It is one that affects the way you show up in life and who you can become. Your ability to learn has an impact on your effectiveness, productivity, and general well-being. Learning to learn is more of an emotional competency than an intellectual one; the emotions most needed to develop it are courage and openness. Courage is addressed in detail earlier in the book as one of the ESE competencies. Related to the emotion of courage is openness, described below.

Openness is the emotional predisposition that allows you to try on new ideas and new situations—not to necessarily agree with them, but to be willing to receive and explore them without immediately judging or dismissing them. Openness for the coach means listening in such a compassionate way that any assessments (or judgments) you make are at the service of the client in his or her process of learning, exploring, reflecting, and questioning. Both openness and courage are required to learn.

As a coach aspiring to excellence, it is important for you to do your own self-assessment around your competence at learning to learn. How good are you at learning? What mood do you typically bring to a new learning situation? Do you know how to design learning? What do you do when you realize that you aren't competent to generate a desired outcome and you don't know what actions to take? How do you prepare yourself to learn? Do you blame yourself for not knowing? What happens to your self-regard when you realize you have something to learn? How ambitious are you about learning to become a great coach?

The learning to learn competency is one of the most fundamental skills needed in today's rapidly changing world. It is your most effective resource to deal with the phenomenon of change, both for yourself, with your clients, and within your organization. Adapting to changing life conditions will be easier for those who have the competencies to expand their learning continuously.

In Newfield's work in coaching individuals and organizations over the last three decades, we have discovered that there are common enemies to learning that limit effectiveness and well-being. The list is long, but some of the favorites among the managers and leaders we teach are: "I don't grant you authority to teach me," "I don't have time," "I can't learn this, given who I am," and so on. The applicable enemy of learning for this book is that most of the time, emotions are left out of the territory of learning. Our culture's current common sense about what learning is causes us to privilege learning things, facts, and information over learning the emotions needed to have better relationships.

Here is a practice that you can do to apply this to your own life (and that of your clients). As before, this practice is best done in a quiet and reflective space. Take out a piece of paper and write down what occurs to you from these questions:

- What is it that you most need to learn at this time in your life to achieve your desired results? (Be careful not to rush to an answer, but really explore possibilities.)
- Now, given that is what you most need to learn, what is the emotion(s) that you need to learn in order to do that? (Again, don't rush to the answer, but let the question steep within you.)

We rarely think about the emotions we need to learn in order to go about more effective and meaning-filled living. Recently, an experienced coach asked for coaching because she felt she had tried everything to grow her practice but yet nothing was working. The Newfield coach did the exercise above with her and what the client discovered was that she really wanted to learn how to declare herself satisfied. She actually was making enough money, but one of her unexamined assumptions was that you can always do better and have more. Learning to be satisfied and declare that you have or are enough requires more than just a cognitive insight. It also requires learning new emotions such as courage, peace, a valuing of self, and compassion, just to name a few. It is a direct result of developing the ESE capability of living with authentic success.

Let's look at an example of a coach working with her clients, John and Sara, to help them discover how empowering this concept of learning to learn can be. This coach developed her own ability to learn how to learn well so that she is capable of assisting her clients in building this skill.

John and Sara constantly argued about their spending habits and never having enough money at the end of the month to put into their retirement account. Month after month, year after year, they took the same actions and produced the same results, with which they were never happy. When asked by their coach why it took eleven years to admit they needed to learn something new in order to take care of their financial concerns, their reply was that they had never thought about their problem in terms of learning. They had always considered it as that was simply the way their relationship was—that's how they *were*—and never saw it as an opportunity to learn so that new choices, actions, or outcomes became possible. One of the greatest gifts their coach gave them was the fact that there was actually nothing wrong with them—they were not flawed human beings, nor did they have anything to be ashamed of or to hide. They simply needed to learn.

Historically, we have not considered emotions important to the learning context or the content. We have rarely considered that some emotions might actually predispose us to learning more effectively or easily. We haven't recognized that some emotions might be necessary for learning to ever happen at all.

One of the enemies of learning for John and Sara was the emotional context in which they viewed their problem. They were ashamed of their problem and of themselves in that "should" they have been smarter, they would not have had their problem in the first place. The coach was able to reveal and challenge the emotional context in which they perceived this issue and encouraged them to see that new learning was needed. The coach, through her own emotional awareness and presence, generated a safe space for conversation so in the dialogue the couple could explore new actions to take without blame. The coach brought to the coaching conversations the emotions of self-regard, acceptance, openness, curiosity, and excitement at the possibility of the couple achieving their financial goals. The coach specifically had the couple practice conversations about money and then pointed out when their language and emotions drifted to blame and shame, as opposed to possibility and curiosity.

As a coach, examining how it is you define, approach, and carry out learning for yourself is critical. Great coaches are life learners and, as we've discussed here, learning includes the territory of emotions. To practice this strategy of learning to learn, one useful exercise is to identify the emotional competencies you will need for the learning task ahead and to do an honest self-assessment as to whether you have that emotional competence or whether you need to learn new emotions to better serve your learning process.

# 3. EMOTIONAL IMMERSION

"Because our minds seek one another through limbic resonance, because our physiologic rhythms answer the call of limbic regulation, because we change one another's brains through limbic revision—what we do inside relationships matters more than any other aspect of human life" (Lewis, Amini, & Lannon, 2000, p. 192).

In the book, *A General Theory of Love*, from which that insight comes, the authors assert that perhaps one of the biggest errors in the early development and practice of therapy was that therapists were trained to keep their emotional distance from the patient out of the fear that the patient would become attached in unhealthy ways to the therapist. Ironically, what they discovered in the scientific research was that the resonant connection that developed between their limbic brains was perhaps the most healing part of the relationship between patient and therapist. Their limbic brains actually sought to guide both parties into increasingly deep and meaningful levels of connection through nonverbal resonance, without any conscious awareness or effort on the part of either party.

New scientific research confirms that in emotionally effective coaching the coach must consciously create the emotional context that is necessary for the client to explore the possibilities of new thinking and new actions. In fact, this is a key competence not only in coaching but in leading. It is a skill that you, the coach, can and must learn to be able to work effectively with your clients.

Imagine the leader of a production team who has fallen into the emotion of resentment because the last quarter production goals were missed. Resentment is the emotion that results from his refusal to accept this unpleasant but unchangeable fact. But without the awareness that he's fallen into resentment, and without learning practices that will help him rediscover his ability to observe the situation from a place where he can accept the current conditions as something he can change over time, he won't be able to recover the motivation and ambition he needs to inspire the team to a new level of success and greatness.

The emotional context from which you coach is intimately connected to the outcomes you and your client or team will generate. Throughout this book, you've read about emotional competencies and practices to generate a wider emotional range. Perhaps the most simple, and at the same time hardest, practice for emotional learning is what we call emotional immersion. This is a practice whereby you immerse yourself in the emotional world you most want to learn.

You want to learn gratitude? Immerse yourself in contexts in which gratitude is practiced. You want to learn enthusiasm? Immerse yourself in communities, conversations, relationships, where enthusiasm is present. In fact, great coaches will question clients as to the communities and contexts and conversations in which they spend the most time in an attempt to have the clients evaluate whether those conversations are serving the people they want to become and the outcomes they are trying to achieve.

A simple example is Tom, who was financially successful and the only senior from his small high school graduating class to go on to college. He went to law school and started a small but budding environmental law practice and was now considering a move into local politics. His high school buddies still lived and worked on the family farms in the town where they all grew up together.

Through the coaching relationship, Tom realized that his frequent visits back home with his buddies weren't as fulfilling as they once were. The conversations he found himself in with his friends often devolved into rantings against the things he personally stood for. Tom's coach suggested the practice of immersing himself in conversations and emotional contexts that would support his growth into this new role. Tom subsequently found and joined a political watchdog group with a bent for environmental concerns. Tom's coach also helped him develop other practices for learning to generate the emotions of self-regard and assertiveness that he would also surely need in the political game he was planning to play.

As a coach, you can provide an enormous value to your clients by having them take a look at the conversational spaces in which they are emotionally immersed. You can provide enormous value to yourself by doing the same.

Here's a simple but revealing practice. Write on a sheet of paper a list of the communities and relationships you spend the most time in. (You might list your work, your spouse, your children, your church, your men's group, your book club, your best friend, etc. If you have a list longer than fifteen, then "overwhelmed" is probably something you are very familiar with.) Next to each community or relationship, write down the one or two predominant emotions that are most present there. Now take a look at the list. Is there a theme or pattern of emotions that show up? Does that support you in who you want to become or in accomplishing your goals? If so, how? If not, what do you now see might be possible if you immersed yourself in other communities or relationships? Now take a look at each community or relationship separately. What emotional context is provided for in that community or relationship? Does it serve you? If not, what can you do about it?

Another practice related to this one is to sit quietly for twenty minutes and then write down in free-flow form all the emotions you most need to learn in order to move toward your goals and dreams. (If you aren't clear about this, just ask your closer friends, associates, and family members. They already know what emotions you habitually fall into and which would better serve you.) Is it Ambition? Gratitude? Passion? Self-Regard? Courage? Empathy? Carry the list with you wherever you go and begin to look for people and places where those emotions are present. By doing this you'll soon start to pay more attention to the emotional content of the conversations you find yourself in and will also be continuing to build your emotionally responsive awareness. This is the foundation for then living your life so you genuinely feel you are authentically successful.

## 4. THE ART OF GENTLE IRREVERENCE IN COACHING: A TALE OF TWO COACHES

Coach Sara is chained to her way of seeing reality. Her thinking is embedded in the traditional paradigm of learning and she doesn't know to question it; after all, she has the *right* way. She is caught by rationality and linear thinking and desperately seeks to get her clients into action before the paint on the issues they present is even dry. She looks for causes and effects in her clients' stories and isn't much help to them, even though the clients may feel a little better just by the simple fact that they had a chance to articulate their concerns out loud and hear themselves think. She has no room to allow for the magic, mystery, the illogical, and the non-linear to show up in the coaching conversation. Her definition of success in coaching is to make sure she helped the client solve the issue.

Coach Ken is chained to his way of seeing reality. He dismisses the rational and the traditional and also has no tolerance for opinions and world views that don't align with his own. He doesn't bother with action steps or new learning practices; he has his clients express how they feel and what their intuition is *really* telling them. He has his clients put positive affirmation notes on their bathroom mirrors because he knows that if you "intend" something hard enough, you'll attract it. He is trapped in his own way of seeing the world and will only be of limited help to his clients, but at least they have a chance to articulate their concerns out loud and hear themselves think.

While these may be extremes, and said somewhat tongue-in-cheek, they do illustrate a sampling of what is being called coaching out there in the marketplace. In both cases the coach is limited by his or her own understanding of reality and by his or her habitual way of seeing and doing life.

A good coach smells this trap and brings to the coaching relationship perhaps *the* most essential ingredient for masterful coaching: gentle irreverence. This chapter is focused on bringing you additional ideas and practices for capacities in implementing the five ESE strategies. Learning the art of gentle irreverence will not only enhance your own ESE, but will serve your coaching of others exponentially.

We describe gentle irreverence as the capacity to laugh at your own nonsense—and the nonsense of others—without judgment, since really we all are brilliant at the nonsense. Gentle irreverence is the capacity to be suspicious of any "reasons" you tell yourself why you haven't achieved what you are seeking to achieve. It is the capacity to be suspicious of yourself when you fall into having answers for your clients' concerns. It is the capacity, in the most intense coaching conversation, to have a good laugh, not out of disrespect but because you truly see the clients' expression and exploration of their concerns as opportunities for new learning . . . nothing less, nothing more.

The practice of gentle irreverence takes courage, enormous compassion, and especially lightness, because you are tampering with sacred cows of explanations and reasons for why things are the way they are. Yet, through honing this skill, you will begin to see the stories and reasons as what they truly are—traps in language and understanding that keep you stuck.

So how do you develop your capacity for gentle irreverence? There are a couple of practices we can recommend that at first may seem a little unorthodox, but through years of experience we know they work.

First, start laughing. The fastest way to lighten up is to begin laughing. What makes you smile? What brings you good humor? Visit your local comedy shows, watch comedians on TV, read your favorite comic strips, watch children at play, re-watch your funniest movies. There are even laughter workshops in which participants learn how to belly laugh. Even when there is nothing in particular to laugh at, the art of engaging the physiology and body in a state of laughter dramatically shifts mood.

Second, make a list of all your sacred cows. What are your non-negotiable rules for living? For some they will only wear a certain style of clothing or a particular hairstyle. For some, getting anything less than an A is unthinkable. For another it might be not trying anything new in public, where one could be assessed as stupid or incompetent. What are your sacred cows? Now, here's the hard part: pick one and start toying with it. Start breaking some of your rules. A senior coach we recently worked with on burnout had so many rules for living that she had put herself into the doctor's office with exhaustion. One of her sacred cows was that she took on any client who could pay her fee. Her coach worked with her in identifying her ideal client and had her say no to all others. This wasn't the only sacred cow this coach started tampering with. It wasn't long before she declared a six-week sabbatical and went to the Caribbean to learn scuba diving (and broke another of her sacred-cow rules of never being caught dead in a swimsuit at the age of fifty-two).

To be honest, after training executive and life coaches for more than fifteen years, Newfield has found that the art of gentle irreverence is one of the hardest emotional competencies to learn. Related to the Bar-On measure, gentle irreverence maps to higher scores in self-actualization, empathy, optimism, and reality testing, and all build to the ESE of authentic success. The coach must build a trusting, safe, respectful, yet provoking, conversational space that provides the clients the challenges and the freedom to explore new ideas, thoughts, beliefs, and actions in a way they haven't done before.

To understand the application of this skill, let's review how a coach, experienced both personally and professionally in using gentle irreverence, works with her client, Bob.

Bob was highly valued and positively assessed in his organization. He hired a coach to become more effective at project management, as he had his sights on the most senior position in his organization. His coach asked Bob whether she could interview his stakeholders. She was suspicious of the goal he had set for himself because by every indication she saw—the battery of assessment instruments his organization had him take, his performance appraisals, the awards on his office wall, his rank and title at a fairly young age—he had proven himself very effective at what he did.

The coach interviewed six stakeholders, including peers, customers, and the boss. What was revealed through the conversations was not a need for Bob to develop more productivity or effectiveness at managing projects. What was consistently reported by those stakeholders was that, in order to become the inspiring leader they knew he was capable of being; he would need to attend more to the relationships with his stakeholders. His conversations with them, while extremely efficient and effective, were missing connection and care. He was a content expert, but his relationships were utilitarian at best. He saw conversations as a way to exchange necessary information for the sake of achieving the goal, but not as an opportunity to create trust, loyalty, friendship, and connection. His stakeholders wanted him to genuinely care about how they were doing—as human beings—not just as means to an end.

Bob's coach didn't buy his initial goal of wanting to be a more effective project manager, and yet Bob insisted that having increased effectiveness was his goal. Bob didn't initially understand what the stakeholders were talking about, and he didn't have another way to observe or see relationships in the workplace. It took Bob's coach several coaching conversations to win Bob's trust before the coach could revisit the stakeholder comments and explore Bob's relationships with others as a potential area for development. In addition to building trust, Bob's coach was exceptional at introducing ideas and topics with great lightness. The coach introduced the stakeholder concerns with complete wonder and curiosity, rather than as a criticism, condemnation, or invalidation of Bob's competence. Bob's coach would find opportune times in the conversations to weave relationship building in with being better at project management. As one of Bob's homework assignments, the coach had Bob spend a little extra time in every conversation he had with his stakeholders on non-work-related issues. At first Bob reported it felt artificial and superficial. As he grew his emotional capacities for care and connection and empathy, he found he enjoyed the conversations, and his stakeholders reported a shift in his ability to connect and inspire. He was building his ESE skills in valuing others, which supported developing his skills in authentic success.

In addition to the coach not buying Bob's story about needing to get better at project management, she also embodied and modeled for Bob a way of being in a relationship in a very different way than Bob was accustomed to. The coach was thoughtful, trusting, wildly curious, at times even playful, and obviously more committed to Bob's success than to pleasing him.

As a coach, two great questions as you engage with your client are: Am I pleasing this client, or am I serving this client through gentle irreverence? Am I trying to come off as brilliant or intelligent, or am I bringing all my intelligences (cognitive, emotional, and somatic) to be of service to this client? You might even want to consider posting these two questions near the workspace where you coach.

## SUPPORTING YOUR SKILLS

Last but not least, we recommend that you become a member of the International Coach Federation as another way for the coaches reading this book to maintain a high standard of coaching skills and competencies. The ICF is a nonprofit membership organization and the largest worldwide resource for business and personal coaches, with more than 12,000 members in eighty countries. Among its greatest accomplishments to date is the development of ethics and standards as well as core coaching competencies for the professional coach. The ICF credential is becoming more and more recognized around the world by individuals and organizations looking for higher standards and ethics in the coaches they select. You can visit the ICF's website for more details at www.coachfederation.org.

Unfortunately, much of the coaching today is being practiced by the un-credentialed and un-trained, who are offering traditional consulting, training, and pop-psychology advice under the guise of "coaching." One of the biggest challenges facing the coaching profession today is that anyone can call him- or herself a coach, whether credentialed or not, whether they have any training as a coach, and whether or not they are competent.

By supporting the ICF and the standards and ethics, you support the profession of coaching as a whole, and you also call on those who are representing themselves as coaches to seek a minimum of training and experience and to operate within strict ethical guidelines.

In this chapter, we offered additional strategies and practices for building your emotional competencies, both personally and professionally. We'd like to add that there is no shortcut for learning emotional intelligence. Awareness plus new practices, which this chapter and book have offered, will be the building blocks of new habits in action. And this will take time.

Effective coaches, and ontological coaches in particular, assist the client in the process of challenging the intellectual and emotional blindness that comes from *unexplored assumptions* and habitual ways of thinking and acting. They work with the whole human being, not just the conceptual or cognitive side, and include emotions (and body) as territories for learning.

We encourage you to incorporate some, if not all, of these strategies into your own personal development plan so that the emotional context that you coach from can hold all the possibilities for your clients to manifest their greatness.

# FOUR

# Case Studies

Part Four contains two chapters that present several case examples of building ESE awareness and capabilities through coaching. Chapter Ten is contributed by guest writer Lee Salmon. As a federal leader in coaching, Salmon presents an overview of the importance of coaching to bring out EI competencies in government leaders. He addresses examples from several different types of federal agencies and explains the importance of developing ESE to respond to the challenges of the change in structure federal agencies experienced when they reduced their middle management staff and to meet the great challenge the federal government is facing as so many senior leaders retire in the next few years.

The final chapter is collaboratively developed with one case example each from Newfield Network and Collaborative Growth. The first example, provided by Newfield Network, discusses the challenges of a CEO in a family business. Recognizing that the challenges were system-wide, the wise coach refused to coach the CEO in isolation. Through work with the coach, every board member learned to build his or her emotional awareness and capabilities and to challenge and change habitual ways of speaking and interacting that were hurting the company.

The second example, provided by Collaborative Growth, presents the learning opportunities of an up-and-coming leader who is also a mother of three. She moved fast at everything she did and didn't waste any time on chit chat. She began to recognize more about how she felt and why through the coaching conversations and to get to know the others she worked with much better. They felt her increased attentiveness, and that was to everyone's benefit.

# Coaching to Enhance, Develop, and Strengthen Emotional and Social Competencies in Government Leaders

*Contributed by Guest Author
G. Lee Salmon, Federal Consulting
Group, U.S. Department
of the Treasury\**

Coaching to develop emotional effectiveness skills in government leaders has become increasingly critical over time. Agencies face continuing cuts in their budgets, loss of senior staff due to retirements, and the increasingly

---

\* The views expressed in this article are those of the author and do not reflect the official policy or view of the Bureau of Public Debt, the Treasury Franchise Fund, or the U.S. Department of Treasury.

complex nature of work requiring collaboration and social intelligence skills. Most executives and managers in leadership positions were promoted based on their technical competence, not on their people skills. Competence in the emotional and social effectiveness (ESE) skills described in this book is proving essential for effective public sector leadership.

In 1995 the federal government went through a period of significant downsizing as part of the Reinventing Government programs of the Clinton Administration. First-line and middle management levels were targeted for reduction and the span of control of managers was increased. At this time government also was beginning to move to a team-based work environment to deal with the growing complexity of problems and issues related to accomplishing agency missions.

The demands for organizational accountability for business results and the socially dynamic nature of teams meant that everyone had to learn how to communicate more effectively and develop ESE skills. With fewer managers left in the management chain, it became even more essential to support the development of the skills and talents of front-line managers and to provide clearer, more effective communication and delegation of authority and responsibility.

Meg Wheatley, author of *Leadership and the New Science*, observed that real power and energy are generated through relationships in organizations, and that patterns of relationships and the capacities to develop them are important, even more so than tasks, functions, roles, and positions (1994). This was a difficult challenge for many scientific and technical organizations in which managers were more valued and rewarded for their technical expertise—and not their relationship management skills.

The nature of leadership also began to change. The skills to lead and motivate teams were minimally present in most managers. The need for a clearer distinction between good management skills and one's capacity for leadership needed to be elucidated. The concept of leadership at all levels began its nascent emergence as the concern for how work was done became as important, if not more so, than the technical substance of the work itself. People were expected to take initiative and step up and lead when required and not wait for a manager's approval. This pointed to the need to improve emotional intelligence skills across all levels of the organization.

During the mid-1990s, coaching was gaining a strong foothold in the private sector as an effective way of developing leadership talent, but it was only available to a select few at the highest executive levels in government. Coaching at that time also often carried the stigma of being only for those who were in trouble, whose careers were derailing, and it was viewed as a strategy of last resort. With its relatively high cost, there was a great demand to show how it could provide a good return on investment. Certainly saving the careers of high-priced senior executives and avoiding the large costs of recruiting and training their replacements made a good case for the investment.

Succession planning in government became an important concern late in the 1990s when demographic studies showed an aging workforce in which a wave of baby boomer retirements would begin early in the 21st century. Currently, there are about 1.9 million people working in the federal government, and a recent study says, "Much has been written about the expected wave of federal retirements, especially among supervisors and managers. The average federal employee is forty-six years old and getting older, and almost 60 percent of federal employees are older than forty-five, compared to 40 percent in the private sector. According to OPM and Partnership estimates, about 550,000 federal employees will leave the government in the next five years (by 2011), the majority through retirement (Partnership for Public Service, 2007, p. 4). Thus, the need to develop leadership talent is rapidly rising to a crisis point. Coaching is now seen as one of the more effective ways of developing leadership and emotional and social effectiveness skills. It is already an integral part of virtually all government Senior Executive Service Candidate Development Programs, and a growing part of agency leadership development programs.

When coaching federal workers it is important to keep in mind the system in which they are working. Of course, this will be true for any coachee. What's different from executives in the private sector is that federal leaders need to build and integrate two powerful emotional muscles. The first is acceptance—the system is embedded in its type of thinking and its structure, including the civil service system, laws, and cultural expectations and norms, impacts what's possible. The second is ambition—so the system is accepted without that leading to resignation or resentment, so that innovation can show up in spite of the systemic issues and in the context of what is possible within the system. Too often innovation dies with federal career executives who lose their energy to "fight" the system anymore. Their resignation will permeate their leadership. They will resort to doing "more of the same," with only peripheral improvements here and there. Too often this goal of minor tweaking becomes the focus, while the coachee awaits retirement or the next promotion. No matter what agency the coachee is working in, it is; therefore, important to keep the context he or she is serving in mind and to help him or her find viable ways to move forward while sustaining energy and creativity. If the coach treats the system as if it "should" be the same as private industry, the coach's work can be harmful and lead to resignation.

The following case studies demonstrate innovative ways that coaching has been used to develop ESE skills in executives and managers in agencies across the federal government.

## COACHING IN THE INTELLIGENCE COMMUNITY

In 2001 leaders in the intelligence community realized that the lessons learned from the September 11, 2001, World Trade Center catastrophe created challenges for the development of future leaders. The lack of effective communication and coordination between agencies within the community that prevented identification and interdiction of the terrorists pointed to the need to develop new skill sets in intelligence officers. The need to collaborate more effectively in their relationships with each other and their counterparts in other agencies was critical; yet turf issues and protection of sources made this a difficult challenge. Resolving it would require realizing a greatly expanded loyalty and a more inclusive sense of responsibility. This was a call to grow the emotional and social effectiveness of an entire culture—one steeped in secrecy and control.

In 2003, a leadership development program was created in one agency involved in human intelligence collection. The program was designed for high-potential, top-level officers. The goal was to strengthen and expand their leadership competencies, especially in the areas of emotional effectiveness, which requires greater self-awareness and interpersonal communication skills. This program was specifically designed as an incubator wherein highly competent officers could develop authentic leadership skills and become viable candidates for new Senior Intelligence Service (SIS) executive positions.

The program's cohort of twenty-five officers worked on a number of innovative, important team and individual projects that required courageous communications to help resolve long-standing challenges within the agency. The glue that connected the various aspects of the program throughout its twelve-month duration was the executive coaching team. Each participant was assigned an executive coach to help support and guide his or her development throughout the program.

The coach helped his or her clients create a customized path for the development of authentic leadership skills and abilities. By working to increase their self-awareness and build skills in the five domains of ESE, the clients were able to see more clearly how their actions affected others and understand how to clarify communication and improve interpersonal responsiveness. They worked together to develop a plan to develop new emotional behaviors needed to seek and to give high-quality feedback.

In 2004, under the National Intelligence Reform and Terrorism Protection Act, the Office of the Director of National Intelligence (ODNI) was created to coordinate activities across the sixteen agencies comprising the national intelligence community. In October 2005, the National Clandestine Service was created to be responsible for the coordination of all human intelligence activities, including those in the CIA, FBI, and Pentagon. Members of the NCS were not accustomed to working effectively together; each entity had its own areas of competence, turf, and power—with prejudices that often excluded communication and coordination with other agencies, except in the most perfunctory manner.

Clearly the ODNI had to break through this cultural logjam to create a level playing field in which robust information sharing and coordination among all community members was expected. The criticality of becoming a community team player was never more important, and the first director, John Negroponte, and his deputy, General Michael Hayden (later the director of the CIA), laid this out in a series of communications with senior intelligence community leaders. As an example, there is now a requirement that anyone who wants to become a Senior Intelligence Service executive must have at least one tour of duty in an agency other than his or her own.

As a result, the importance of developing the emotional effectiveness skills necessary for creating partnerships, collaboration, and coordination across the intelligence community became an even more focused part of leadership development.

In interviews with the leadership coaching team about areas of development for their clients, a number of emotional effectiveness skill areas were mentioned:

- Centering and the ability to be fully present in the moment (Responsive Awareness)
- Willingly seeking out regular feedback from and giving constructive feedback to others on a more frequent basis (Valuing Yourself and Others)
- Managing fear and marshalling courage during times of conflict and crisis (Courage)
- Understanding how and where emotions reside in the body (Responsive Awareness)
- Managing one's emotions for power and influence (Valuing Yourself)
- Developing stronger connections with others by understanding how one's mood can affect the quality of relationships (Valuing Others)

As a team coach, one of my clients learned through 360-degree feedback that in contentious meetings with her sister agency counterparts, she tended to become very quiet, appeared to withdraw, and was pushed around by people with more dominant personalities. At first she discounted these perceptions, but she became more receptive to considering them when a close friend indicated that he had observed the same behavior in another meeting with her boss. The boss tended to be very demanding in pushing his agenda. In that situation, she again appeared to cave in and not stand up for herself.

As her coach, I helped her begin a process of self-observation that enabled more awareness of her body responses and feelings during emotionally intense encounters. I helped her learn how to center herself and regain balance when she felt under attack. Another coach and I worked with her to develop a series of centering and relaxation practices based on martial arts and neuro-linguistic programming (NLP) techniques that she could practice on her own. I slowly worked to help build her confidence and competence in managing her emotions so she could stay present during conflict and be able to appropriately confront and engage others.

Another client was a deputy manager. At times he not only performed his own job but also that of another operations person whose slot was unfilled for some time. He had an impossibly demanding, stressful job that was affecting his health and family life.

He tended to have strong inflexible opinions and believed he knew how the organization should be run, so he often clashed with his boss around policy and direction. This led to tension and a lack of trust between them that strained their professional relationship and undermined the confidence of staff in some of his decisions.

Conducting a 360-degree survey using structured interview questions produced a greater understanding of the office dynamics and how the staff and the group chief perceived the deputy's effectiveness in his position. The results revealed that everyone had high regard for his honesty, integrity, and dedication to mission. He worked hard and was very knowledgeable, yet some of the staff saw him as a choke point. Approvals to release vital communications or operational plans languished for days on his desk. He was so busy he had little time to meet with staff, and when he did he would multi-task by doing other things during their conversations.

The group chief saw him as a loose cannon who would countermand her decisions, second-guess her, and not directly voice policy disagreements. She simply didn't trust him to work with her as a partner. Her lack of trust developed because of his unawareness of his own emotions and his attitude of, "I know better than you." He also lacked the courage to speak up strongly when he had a different view of a decision she planned to make, and he would reverse decisions when she was away from the office. These were issues we addressed by focusing on the development of critical ESE skills such as Responsive Awareness, Courage, and Valuing Self.

His challenge was to see and accept the perceptions of others as valid, rather than develop defensive excuses as to why he was right. He needed to learn how to receive critical feedback. Clearly, he had issues around effective delegation, being able to trust his staff, and remaining fully present with staff during meetings. He also had some serious fence mending to do with his boss to regain her trust and find the courage to confront her when they had disagreements on policy decisions. This required further development in the skill of Valuing Others.

We had several discussions about the feedback and how to leverage the strengths identified by his raters. He worked on a specific self-observation exercise when in meetings with his staff. He was to observe whether or not he stopped to get ready in advance for the meeting and whether he was fully present during the meeting. We also discussed the importance of being open to meeting with his boss to share highlights of his feedback and review the progress he was making in developing Responsive Awareness, Valuing Others, and Courage, particularly as pertained to their relationship.

Once he realized that his listening skills needed improvement, we worked on two strategies: (1) setting aside time just before a meeting so he could prepare to participate fully and (2) taking a moment to center himself if someone just dropped in. He practiced using yogic breathing and relaxation techniques that could, with practice, shift him out of his head and into his body in a relatively short period of time. He learned to ask for a minute to finish his work if someone dropped in, and use that time to center himself before beginning a conversation. This practice also helped improve his ability to listen more attentively and connect with his staff.

Within a few months, his boss moved on to a new assignment and that gave him the opportunity to build trust from the beginning with his new boss by using the lessons he had learned. He later reported that he and his new boss really hit it off from the beginning, and he now has a productive relationship with him.

Starting in 2006, we began to use the EQ-i self-assessment instrument as an integral part of the leadership development program to help participants better understand their EQ strengths and areas in which improvement might be desirable. Coaches used these results to help focus developmental discussions toward emotional effectiveness skills building. These skills were further reinforced in workshops where experiential small group exercises were introduced that challenged participants to look at the process they used to problem solve and become aware of how the team organized and led itself.

The groups were challenged to go beyond cognitive thinking, where they were strongest, to using artistic and graphical methods of visualizing problems and solutions. They stretched themselves using skits and drama to present results. All of this was designed to develop new orientations to effective problem solving, leadership, collaboration, and the use of emotion and body as modes of expression.

Throughout the classes, participants were regularly challenged to clarify their personal visions of leadership and to practice sharing them in narrative form by telling their own leadership stories. At the end of each class, participants wrote statements of their leadership visions and presented them to the class. We noticed that with each class these statements became clearer and more robustly expressed an integration of the cognitive and emotional dimensions of leadership. At the conclusion of one class, one intelligence operations officer's powerful holistic vision of how he saw himself as a leader was: "I lead by empowering and inspiring the people around me to strive to be better, to enjoy life and take pride in their work and profession, to set high standards for themselves, to take risks, and not be afraid of failure, to learn and to teach, to love and be loved" He had clearly developed his ESE skills of Valuing Yourself, Courage, and Authentic Success.

## COACHING AT THE DEPARTMENT OF TREASURY

In 2005 the Office of the Comptroller of the Currency (OCC), Department of Treasury decided to embark on a pilot coaching program for their high-performing executives and managers. The OCC charters, regulates, and supervises all national banks. It also supervises the federal branches and agencies of foreign banks.

The six-month program used both OCC internal coaches and external coaches. Some of the outcomes clients experienced after coaching could be directly attributed to increased ESE skills:

- Breakthroughs in achievement of personal and organizational goals (Authentic Success)
- Ability to create and lead from a vision (Authentic Success)
- Creation of a high-performance team (Valuing Others)
- Increased self- and organizational awareness (Responsive Awareness)
- Greater ability to learn and take action (Valuing Self)
- Ability to manage upward (Courage)
- Enhanced partnering and collaboration (Valuing Others)

In a recent testimonial to the value of the coaching experience, one regional district manager remarked that he felt overwhelmed and realized that he could no longer manage the banks under his jurisdiction in the same way he had in the past, given the mandated consolidation of field offices within his district. His coach challenged him to rethink his management style and identify ways to give more responsibility to junior staff. She helped him develop interpersonal communication skills, which meant more meetings by phone and fewer meetings in person. He also was asked to train junior analysts to handle details he once performed personally. His coach helped him get in touch with the emotional sense of loss in not being able to meet personally as often with his customers. He had enjoyed the customer interface; it gave him a sense of accomplishment. The coach helped him reframe this loss by expanding his definition of what it meant to provide good customer service.

Through peer and senior manager feedback, the manager recognized the necessity to make more time to take a greater leadership role in an important senior committee. His coach helped him understand that this would require better time management and delegation of responsibilities to others to free up time for these greater leadership responsibilities. To do this, he had to become more self-aware and develop the ability to trust other staff to fill in for him.

His coach helped him practice being able to clearly state his performance expectations and to follow up with conversations about accountability. Through developing the courage to step up to his new committee leadership responsibilities, she helped him to voice the emotional uncertainties he felt about playing a new role through reflection, journaling, and conversation. She also assigned practices for deepening his relationships with other committee members that included asking for their support and periodic feedback. Directly asking his staff for their support during the time it would take to acquire these new leadership skills was another big step.

Another client was a director seeking promotion, but not seen as competent by his supervisor. Whenever he briefed his supervisor, he felt intimidated, which led to his losing track of the subject. He felt that she knew more technically and was prone to judge or question him on technicalities. She also was impatient when he wandered off track.

As his coach, I saw that his personal development needed to focus on building confidence and self-esteem and skills in meeting preparation and agenda control. We needed to build the ESE skills of Responsive Awareness, Valuing Self, and Valuing Others. Together we used a 360-survey instrument to help discover where others saw his strengths and challenges. The results showed that others admired him for his genuineness and compassion, so he built on those strengths, along with his commitment to excellence, and grew to value himself more accurately. Then he began practicing more self-discipline in preparing for meetings with his boss. We also worked on understanding his boss better, which was accomplished through conversations with a mentor who was her peer.

With practice and better meeting preparation, he was able to have more confidence and courage to speak up and make sound and powerfully stated recommendations. At his performance review, his boss remarked on the positive changes she saw in him and eventually approved him to take over a responsible leadership position as an examiner in charge of a large bank.

Other participants in the program without exception made remarks in evaluation interviews about their challenges and what they were able to accomplish in the coaching program (Federal Consulting Group, 2006, pp. 3–5). Highlights of their comments and related ESE skills include:

- I'm more engaged in my job and thinking more creatively about how I handle my responsibilities. I'm taking more time to focus on my division and OCC priorities. I'm spending more time on staff development. (Responsive Awareness)
- I was able to develop a plan, set priorities, and take action on key strategic issues that were languishing because of my lack of awareness and sense of being overwhelmed as a new director. (Responsive Awareness)
- (Coaching) helped mend a broken relationship with my boss by me learning to manage up more skillfully. (Courage)
- I'm better able to deal with problem employees and give feedback more skillfully without alienating people. (Valuing Others)
- (Coaching) helped me develop a strategic action plan on how to make myself more effective. (My coach) helped me hold myself accountable for progress. (Valuing Self)

- (Coaching) helped me see the value of getting up from my desk and walking around talking with my direct reports and building relationships. (Valuing Others)

Each coach used different techniques to build critical emotional effectiveness skills necessary for individual and organizational culture change. In the last example, the coach gave his client an assignment to strengthen empathy by simply having him take the time to walk around and talk to his people, something every manager should know, but in the crush of time seldom does consistently. The client had to break through his idea of what was a productive use of his time, challenge his introverted habit of isolating himself in his office, and rethink the assumption that just churning out his work was the best measure of his or *anyone's* productivity.

By its second year, the Treasury program had thirty participants, including senior executives such as deputy comptrollers. More and more federal employees are asking to be coached so they can improve their interpersonal skills, including their emotional and social intelligence.

## LEADERSHIP COACHING AT NASA

The NASA Goddard Space Flight Center (Center) is home to the nation's largest organization of scientists and engineers dedicated to learning and sharing their knowledge of the earth, solar system, and universe. With an ambitious and difficult mission, the Center must grow leaders who can ensure that its people feel a sense of community, connection, collaboration, and purpose. It also must have managers who can speak truth to those in power, challenge unclear assumptions affecting the mission, and be prepared for disruptive but critical organizational changes that may be made during times of uncertainty. Clearly, coaching for emotional effectiveness is critical in helping these leaders meet challenges of this nature.

In 2001 coach Joan Wangler, president of EDIN Associates, met with a group of self-selected leaders from Goddard's Project Management Development Enterprise and launched a community of practice that evolved into a creative learning group called Mission: Space to Grow (Bamberger & Bradley, 2005; Wangler, 2007). Six years later, the learning groups have flourished in the organization and spread to other agencies, including the Environmental Protection Agency and the Departments of Health and Human Services, Agriculture, and Commerce. Joan says, "It is all about informal learning, people talking about what matters in their lives—in their homes and on the job—sharing experiences, having courageous conversations, and creating powerful relationships for mutual support and action" (Wangler, p. 1). The point is to apply the substance of those discussions and make effective changes.

The learning groups meet twice a month for coaching and facilitated learning conversations. Other coaches and resources are brought in to stimulate thinking. The learning groups then sponsor workshops to expand thinking and exploration. Sometimes representatives from other federal agencies take part in the workshops, helping to break down communication barriers and facilitate dialogue between agencies. Leadership coaching expands from one-on-one to department, agency, and inter-agency-wide applications.

At NASA the learning group conversations have become the fuel for enlivening the workplace and producing outstanding work, as demonstrated by their improved collaboration. Mission: Space to Grow members have developed a network of trust by coaching and mentoring each other and transferring these communication skills to other employees. The group has radically galvanized learning, knowledge sharing, and organizational change, taking the concept of coaching to a highly creative level.

Mission: Space to Grow provides a tipping point for other learning groups to take shape, expanding to include members from different directorates at Goddard. All the learning groups meet together for Center-wide education. By working closely with one another, with their coach, and with special guest coaches, members can view themselves more realistically, see their blind spots, connect with a new-found personal wisdom, consider new possibilities, collaborate, and take new action. This supports the development of the ESE skills of Responsive Awareness, Valuing Yourself, Valuing Others, and Authentic Success.

Coaching, emotional intelligence, principles of appreciative inquiry, somatic work, and other cutting-edge practices are introduced to the Goddard employees. Implementing these benefits requires enhancing the emotional effectiveness skills of members, particularly with the skills of Responsive Awareness and Valuing Self and Others.

One member of the learning community had a remarkable insight stimulated by his group experience. While in a conversation about the value of doing meaningful work, he realized that his motivation for work was: "Civil servants deliver America's dream."

This insight changed his perspective on work and influenced the way he managed because he now tapped deeper into using the ESE skills of Responsive Awareness, Valuing Yourself, and Valuing Others. He said, "I use the learning group as a model for my operation and believe to the extent to which I can establish a safe environment, the more productive we are as an organization. People feel more confident about their own ideas, challenging the way we've done things historically. The learning group provides a foundation for dialogue and for dealing with conflict constructively. The answers are in the group; at any one time we are all leaders. . . . We will have greater buy-in, be more productive, and able to impart these messages to others on the team to the extent we are able to collaborate to address problems and our strategic goals" (Wangler, p. 8).

Another group member reported: "The tools that I learned taught me to not only understand and use my own strengths and limitations more effectively, but to be more understanding of other colleagues, particularly under situations of conflict and stress. I am more aware of the fact that each worker is a human being and that 'problems' are really just 'situations' that we need to address" (Wangler, p. 11). The ability to become responsive and aware of the feelings of others and to be empathetic during times of stress are skills needed for effective leadership in any organization.

The necessity to coach people to find courage to speak truth to power was articulated by one group member who observed that when the Challenger shuttle disaster occurred, it was clearly diagnosed as a failure to communicate with the engineers: "They knew those 0-rings were going to fail, they raised the issues, but did not have the communication skills, or the social capital, to have that message heard." He went on to say, "I believe that when the kinds of conversations that take place within learning groups are the norm, when issues like that arise they will be heard. Once you are holding yourself accountable at a high level, then you get to ask the organization to do the same—there's enormous leverage. . . . It gives you the courage to hold the rest of the organization accountable—people have a platform from which to do that" (Wangler, p. 18).

With the Columbia shuttle disaster, it was clear that NASA had a culture that didn't expect engineers to speak up and defend safety issues. "As the Columbia Accident Investigation Board examined the incident, they found that the behavior of many of the managers and engineers during the Columbia tragedy reflected the cultural norms and deeply ingrained patterns of behavior that had existed for years at NASA. The organization had operated according to hierarchical procedures and strict rules of protocol for as long as the shuttles had been flying. Communication often followed a strict chain of command, and engineers rarely interacted directly with senior managers, who were several levels higher in the organization. Status differences had stifled dialogue for years (Roberto, 2005, p. 65). Coaching at an individual and group level was required to change this norm.

## LEADERSHIP COACHING AT THE EPA

At the Environmental Protection Agency the learning group concept was adapted to create incubators for the development of authentic leadership through coaching in small and large groups. EPA's Office of Research and Development began an organizational improvement effort in 1995 to provide better science linked to environmental priorities. Group and individual coaching began to be introduced in 2002 to help managers improve their leadership and emotional and social effectiveness skills.

Around the same time, in the EPA Office of Pesticides, Prevention, and Toxic Substances, its senior leader, who then became the EPA administrator, championed leadership learning groups for managers and high-potential staff. These groups were based on the NASA experience and used coach facilitators to stimulate provocative conversations. After three years as a successful pilot program, these small diverse groups grew into a larger community forum, a speakers series called Transformational Leadership Conversations: Finding Our Way During Times of Uncertainty. These community events continued to promote the idea of leadership at all levels as part of broad culture change across the whole agency. Mary O'Reilly, a leader of this change work and early champion for these community events, said about NASA and EPA: "Each agency has been very creative, though the models differ; they are heralded as a sound venue for improving motivational levels, positive organizational change and substantive results" (O'Reilly, 2007).

Over the past two years, ten nationally recognized leaders and coaches have spoken to room-capacity audiences and to other EPA staff nationwide using iPTV technology that delivers streaming video to each person's desktop computer. Some of the notable speakers included David Walker, Comptroller General of the United States, from the U.S. Government Accountability Office, Dr. Peter Senge, MIT senior lecturer and founder of the Society for Organizational Learning, and David Gergen, professor and director of the Center for Public Leadership at Harvard University.

At each event leadership coaches and their clients, mentors and protégés, and senior EPA leaders are stimulated by provocative themes, ranging from leadership for environmental sustainability to 21st century leadership challenges facing the federal government. Conversations stimulated at the TLC events often continue afterward, reaching diverse parts of EPA and other federal agencies, thus promoting the effectiveness of group coaching, combined with one-on-one coaching within a community of intentional ESE change. These events generate many opportunities to practice ESE skills such as Responsive Awareness, Courage, and Valuing Others.

Executive coaches enter this arena and begin to work with government and business leaders as partners in learning. The world and human survival may in some small part be dependent on how well we as coaches take a leadership role, using and teaching ESE skills, and modeling emotional and social intelligence. We can help create communities and environments for innovative conversations that push the boundaries of limited thinking, opening new, creative possibilities for global sustainability. Margaret Wheatley said it best: "I believe we can change the world if we start listening to one another again. Simple, honest, human conversation. Not mediation, negotiation, problem solving, debate, or public meetings. Simple, truthful conversation where we each have a chance to speak, we each feel heard, and we each listen well" (Wheatley, 2002, p. 3).

# CHAPTER 11

# Case Examples

## *Marcia Hughes, James Terrell,*
## *Julio Olalla, and Terrie Lupberger*

### BUILDING EMOTIONAL CAPACITY: THE POWER OF MOOD IN A GROUP: A CASE STUDY

#### Background

Danny was a tired and frustrated thirty-five-year-old president of a family-owned company doing approximately $24 million in revenues each year. He was the third-generation president, whose job mainly consisted of bookkeeping, financial oversight, and peacekeeping among the other family owners.

Over the course of the last ten years, he and the four other owners had grown apart, were now living in three separate regions of the country, had three separate offices, and had developed a pattern of ineffectual and gossip-ridden conversation with each passing year. The organization was financially stable, but had not grown in revenues in the last four years. Employee grumbling and dissatisfaction were at an all-time high. At the last owners' meeting, there was a huge disagreement among the owners over future direction of the company, and two owners walked out.

The relationship had devolved to blaming, opinion-making, and posturing, and Danny realized he was caught in a mood of great resignation about the business, seeing little possibility for resolution. As a last resort to try and create something different for the company, he contacted an executive coach to work with him.

## The Coaching Relationship

Danny began by stating that the organization needed team building. The coach, with over ten years of coaching experience, knew not to buy immediately the solution the client was suggesting. After probing with powerful questions about the nature and history of the owners' relationship and the underlying concerns Danny was challenged with, the coach agreed to take Danny on as a coaching client only if Danny and the entire ownership team was willing to work together to discuss concerns and align on moving forward. Yes, the coach could have chosen to work with Danny individually, but the coach knew that by doing so without also looking at the systemic issues and influences that Danny was working within, he would have much less chance at successfully generating the sustainable results he was looking for.

Being an experienced coach trained in facilitating emotional awareness, the coach also recognized that the issues that Danny and the other organizational leaders were facing could not be successfully addressed without building the team's emotional awareness and effectiveness. They needed this increased emotional intelligence to be able to have the difficult but essential conversations to move the organization forward.

Danny was surprised that the company's other owners so quickly agreed to the coaching. They too were frustrated and angry at the inoperability of the working relationship and the potential decline of the business.

The coach started by having each owner take an emotional intelligence assessment. The coach then interviewed five of each owner's primary stakeholders (external customers, internal customers, board members, key employees, and even spouses) to ascertain what the stakeholders thought each owner did very well in their leadership roles and what their biggest learning opportunities were. (Our experience has shown that by interviewing key stakeholders of your coaching clients, you often get a quick and clear picture of the clients' behavioral traits that get in their way of achieving their goals.)

With the feedback from the stakeholders and the results from the emotional intelligence measurement, the coach presented the findings to each owner and discussed what patterns, concerns, frustrations, and learning opportunities the owner saw in the feedback. In that first coaching session, the owner worked with the coach to identify two to three learning goals and action steps they could take in the next six months. The coach asked that one of the learning goals include enhancing the area of emotional awareness that the owner felt was the biggest barrier to a better relationship among the ownership team.

The coach noticed and noted to herself that what had emerged among all the owners' feedback was a pattern of low responsive awareness among this group. This leadership body, as a whole, had low access to noticing what they were feeling or why they were feeling it. As a group, they were more impulsive to jump to conclusions and to blame others for their own mistakes. They also seemed to have low flexibility in seeing others' perspectives, and this was leading to enormous resentment and resignation in the group. No wonder that the organization as a whole was in a stagnant phase. This information helped the coach develop a strategy and framework for getting this group to learn how to better start reading themselves and others in order to make better business choices.

After the initial individual sessions, the coach facilitated a group session with the owners. In this session the coach elicited from each owner his or her biggest frustration in the organization. As an example, one of the owners blamed Danny for fiscal mismanagement. He was frustrated that the company had to pay a higher tax bill this past fiscal year than ever before in the company's history. Danny was handling the books and, according to that owner, "cost them too much money and should have planned better."

Because the owners had spent very little time over the last year actually talking, let alone talking about business issues, Danny didn't know the other owners were upset about this issue. The coach pointed out to the owners that they had fallen out of an important "rhythm" of conversation, they had stopped having recurring and critical conversations necessary for the health of the team and the business. Without these recurring conversations, the owners' habit was to make up their own conclusions and judgments, which fed into the vicious cycle of not wanting to speak with each other.

In the example of blaming Danny and jumping to the conclusion that Danny should have planned better, the coach got the group to see that this conversational move eliminated possibilities for learning, new action, or moving forward as a team. The only move Danny had was to defend or shut down. In that session, the coach got the owner to withdraw his accusation and instead was coached to ask Danny questions that would lead to him having a better understanding of why there was a higher tax bill last fiscal year. This was one step in building that owner's emotional competence of responsive awareness.

Although it began with uncomfortable periods of silence and begrudging commitments at first, by the end of this day-long meeting the context had been set for a different kind of conversation moving forward between the group. The challenge for the coach was demonstrating the courage necessary to hold the conversational space open when the owners wanted to quickly and eagerly go to their familiar patterns of blame and resentment. The coach kept reminding them that this conversational pattern would only produce more of the same and that what they said they most cared about was the health, prosperity, and legacy of the family business.

After this group session, the team spent the next six months working with the coach in bi-weekly, individual coaching sessions, making better requests of each other, being clearer about their expectations and conditions of satisfaction, and practicing clearer communication with each other in their meetings. Over that period of time, the coach worked with each owner on building the owners' own self-awareness (of what they wanted and what they were feeling) and developing a better capacity to listen to the emotions of others. They worked with their coach on identifying their resentment as soon as they noticed it. They practiced conversational moves their coach taught them so that they could listen more deeply and communicate with less judgment.

Danny's coach suggested practices to work on building his emotional awareness. For six months, each day on his way to and from work, Danny drove in silence—no cell phone or radio. It was difficult for Danny at first. The distraction of being busy had taken his mind off his discontent, which he eventually came to realize was a very short-sighted strategy. During these drives he began to have insight into himself and the way he was showing up at work. One of his realizations was that he rarely took the time to acknowledge his staff, so he began the practice of thanking at least one person a day He also realized in one of his reflection times that he had never discussed with the other owners his own vision for the company. In truth, he saw that he did want to be a great leader and with his coach he began to identify the shifts he needed to make in order to show up that way. Through these and other practices and conversations, the coach worked with Danny, and the other team members, to build the ESE application of authentic success.

The six months of individual coaching culminated in a two-day retreat with the owners. The retreat, while not as tense as the first meeting, was still filled with some tension. The longstanding habit of this family and the previous generation of owners was to blame and gossip about the other family members. In this way they could deflect their own responsibility for running the business successfully. Throughout the retreat in which the owners committed to a new shared future and new business practices that would support them in achieving that new future, the coach kept pointing out to the team when they fell back into their old emotional habits.

One of the highlights was that Danny was able to lead a very impactful conversation with one of the other owners who wanted to retire. Danny was able to listen deeply and respectfully without judgment. Without blame or accusation, Danny could hear him and with the others began conversations around ownership changes and new roles in the business.

## Measuring Success

At the beginning of the coaching initiative, the coach had asked each owner what he or she most wanted to learn through the process of coaching. With different words, they all pointed to a desire to have more peace and easiness in their working relationships with each other. At the end of the six-month coaching engagement, the coach had a closing conversation with each owner to assess how well the initial learning goal was met.

Although the specific lessons were different for each of them, they all reported they now had concrete actions they could take to have more powerful and impactful conversations with each other. They all reported experiencing an increase in their emotional capacity—and were somewhat surprised that they hadn't seen what a powerful leadership competency this is. The coach concluded each session by helping each owner design a set of action steps for the learning that each wanted to undertake moving forward.

The coach realized there were two important moves she made in the coaching relationship that set the stage for the client's success. First, she recognized that, while Danny had his own leadership challenges to address, he was also operating within a system that had to be challenged or Danny would have less chance of success. She insisted that in their coaching relationship Danny take a look at those systemic issues as much as his individual leadership challenges.

Secondly, the coach doggedly refused to let the ownership team get away with any assessments of each other when she was in conversation with any of them. This team had inherited a very destructive habit of gossip and blame, and she courageously and consistently pointed to this habit every time she saw it play out. Her commitment was to the team and their developing a new way to lead together. She risked being uncomfortable, she risked having them not like her; she even risked not getting the coaching engagement in the first place. Her courage provided a powerful context for her clients to succeed within.

## DEVELOPING EMOTIONAL AND SOCIAL SKILLS—A CASE STUDY

Bridget enjoys her work for a medical supply company. She's been with them for twenty-two years and has moved up the ranks; a few years ago she was promoted to being the director of the research division for one of their products. Thirty people report to Bridget, who has been identified as a high-potential leader for future promotion. Bridget likes the idea of being promoted, but she doesn't crave it. She entered into coaching when her company offered it to her level of leaders because she's interested in improving her skills as a manager and she was mildly curious. She knows she may or may not be promoted, but that she and her staff could benefit from her improving some of her emotional and social skills. She's a down-to-earth problem solver and, according to Bridget, she doesn't tend to think of emotions as a significant aspect of her work.

know she cared about what was in the team's and their individual best interests. When she took the time to address these more general issues and then explained the context for her requests, she was received better at work and at home. As her assertiveness improved, Bridget became more comfortable in asking for what was needed more promptly. She was learning to not hold herself back out of self-doubt, but rather to speak up confidently before she became so impatient that she sounded uncaring or angry. This allowed her to effectively express her emotions and attend to those of others.

The last goal may have made the biggest difference for Bridget. She started finding little ways to give herself time. As she changed her behaviors, reflected on the changes, and talked quite a bit about them, the processes ceased to feel like homework. Rather, she beamed when she reported week after week that she was arranging her calendar differently so she didn't have to rush. She committed to getting to meetings at least five minutes early instead of rushing in just as they started. This gave her a natural opportunity to talk about interests and feelings with the others in attendance. It created a normal environment for beginning to apply her emotional awareness muscles, and she went for it. In fact, this felt so good she began finding ways to apply it with her children. She would take them to a game a bit early and drive more casually, which gave them time to chat along the way. It was working well, and she committed to continuing to find ways to slow down and invest her time differently. Through the coaching, Bridget began a long-term process of building her ability to value herself and to respond effectively to the emotional as well as programmatic matters raised at work. Similarly, she was developing stronger footing in responding to her children's needs—something that delighted her.

Bridget realized she was much more interested in being a good mom and learning more about her current job than she was in a promotion. She decided she wanted to keep engaged and seek that face time with the executive team when possible, but she understood that moving up the ladder wasn't her priority right now. However, it could be someday and she'd be more prepared by staying in touch.

Geoffrey's insistence in taking time to understand her interests and in helping her become more aware was an important part of the coaching success. He recognized her interest in solving puzzles and subtly characterized the purpose of their coaching process as discovering the picture on

When Geoffrey, her coach, first met Bridget, he found her quite pleasant; however, he was a bit concerned that she seemed to be entering into coaching with minor curiosity, but little passion. She was charming and appeared to be willing to be candid, especially about what she considered her faults to be, but she seemed only moderately invested in making this a growth opportunity. She laughed and said she was bad at doing homework so if he had any she'd give it a try, but he shouldn't count on it.

Bridget indicated she'd recently taken two emotional intelligence questionnaires, the EQ-i® and the EQ 360® in which her boss, direct reports, and peers rated her. Her scores bothered her; she was surprised they were so low. So she saw this coaching as the chance to improve her emotional intelligence. The coaching program design included several meetings in which her supervisor joined them in the coaching session to provide feedback, organizational perspective, and support. While at times a manager's involvement can hinder frankness, in this case it worked well. Bridget and her boss have a positive and trusting relationship. As a matter of fact, her boss had more ambition for her than she did. He seemed to want more out of the coaching process than Bridget was ready for.

Bridget said she only had one goal for the coaching: She would really like to expand her emotional awareness. Her manager, on the other hand, wanted her to improve her positioning so she'd gain more face time with the senior leadership and get a promotion soon. Geoffrey sensed that once he and Bridget had a chance to explore things more openly in coaching sessions that her real interests were likely to unfold with greater clarity and might possibly change considerably. She just needed the chance to access a more trusting and introspective state. The boss's suggestions were relevant, but not controlling of their process.

They worked together for six months, and began by reviewing results from several assessments Bridget had taken over the last year. Geoffrey also asked her to fully describe her current situation as a whole person—on and off work. He invited her to talk about what worked, what didn't work, when she felt challenged, and when she felt strong. Without trying to fix anything, they took time to discover a clear sense of where Bridget wasn't as satisfied with her life as she wanted and felt some real passion to improve. At first her passion was carefully veiled because she believed her life functioned just fine, and she wasn't about to upset the apple cart. She seemed to carefully control how much emotional energy she exhibited.

Geoffrey didn't accept or reject her limited scope for the coaching; rather he asked her to wait until the second session to even start exploring the possible learning goals for their relationship. He said taking more time would facilitate a fresh spirit of inquiry and open learning. Bridget was intrigued. Problem solving was her career, and she was good at it, but now that the "problem" to be fixed had been left open, her inquiring mind began to start noticing parts of her life that she hadn't been noticing. She told her coach about her team, how they were a fairly new division and worked okay together, but she often felt many didn't respect her as their boss. It seemed more like they thought of her as staff right along with them. In response to Geoffrey's questions about how she felt about it, Bridget seemed surprised to begin recognizing her frustration, but she was cautious to make sure her concern didn't get too big. She wanted to stay in control. Geoffrey was beginning to wonder whether they might be working on the ESE skill of valuing self, but he knew he needed to learn more before deciding.

She described the limited access she had to the senior team and her lack of energy about a promotion. She would be happy with one, but. . . . She couldn't put her finger on why it didn't seem exciting, but it didn't. She didn't indicate any fear, just no passion.

Then she talked about her husband and three children. All of a sudden the picture filled out considerably! She had a teenager in high school getting ready for college, one in middle school, and one in elementary school. She and her husband had very demanding professional jobs and didn't believe in getting any more child care help than they really had to. They wanted to be the ones to help their children face their challenges and develop the skills for coping with life. Now Bridget came to life with passion, angst, and funny stories. She started asking for advice on how to coach her ten-year-old perfectionist daughter to lighten up. She wondered how to give the right amount of advice to her high school son so she'd be there for him, but not overdo it. Suddenly, there was traction.

Bridget and Geoffrey found that her EQ-i scores were important indicators of her family challenges as well as work challenges. Bridget had not developed any patterns of paying attention to her own emotions. She knew she cared a lot about issues with her team, but often would take a long time

before she spoke up and then too often blew up with anger for which [she] was quickly sorry. She also felt pushed to make quick decisions whene[ver] someone asked, whether it was one of her children calling for permission [to] participate in a sleepover or a staff person asking for two months' leave f[or a] trip to Egypt. She found it quite interesting that the same behaviors troub[led] her at home and at work. For example, when someone came in her of[fice] and confronted her on a project decision, she felt responsible to ans[wer] immediately and then would often question her rushed decision.

Ultimately, Bridget identified three priorities to work on: impr[ov-]ing her awareness of emotions, talking about them more comfortably [and] willingly, and increasing her assertiveness by learning to give herself m[ore] time and space to respond without needing to rush. Through the coach[ing] process, Bridget raised her interest in knowing more about how she [felt] and she appreciated this time to invest in herself more. Together, she [and] Geoffrey decided that her greatest benefit would come from her focusing [on] responsive awareness. She needed to increase her own awareness of [how] she felt and why and learn how to attend to others more effectively. [They] also decided this work should connect with expanding her sense of val[uing] herself. She felt very good about her problem-solving skills, but was h[old-]ing herself back in engaging with others, such as her team, as her emoti[onal] uncertainty led her to being too deliberate and held her back from show[ing] she cared.

Setting a goal to increase her assertiveness really surprised her. [She] thought she was very assertive, but everyone—boss, peers, and d[irect] reports—rated her low in this competency in her 360 evaluation. She [real-]ized that she was often criticized for being brusque, for speaking in [a] matter-of-fact a way and being too demanding. So she often held bac[k on] asking for what she needed until the need was so compelling that it bec[ame] a serious pressure. This fed the brusque behavior. Her discomfort with e[mo-]tions made her refrain from talking about her joys or concerns and over[look] asking about how others felt. Her assertiveness did need sharpening, [spe-]cifically in combining her feelings with requests and in trusting herse[lf to] speak up sooner. Through the coaching relationship, Bridget learned to [take] time to ask others about how their projects or other parts of their lives w[ere] going. It helped her make more reasonable requests of people. Geof[frey] coached her in using empathic assertiveness. That called for her to let f[eel]

a puzzle that needed time to be assembled. He didn't just emphasize the boss's wishes and encourage her to put all her energy into being promoted. He worked with Bridget to help her understand her current priorities from an emotional as well as a programmatic perspective. Finally, he recognized that her resistance to "homework" came from her demanding home life and helped her discover ways to implement changes and reflection time within the natural flow of life, rather than giving her assignments she'd have to do after the children went to bed or went out for the evening, in the case of the teenager.

Bridget reported at the end of the six months that she had made significant progress and was more peaceful than she'd been for a long time. Her favorite improvement was getting to meetings early so she wasn't rushed and had time to get to know folks. She still talks about that as one of the unexpected benefits she gained from coaching.

# Conclusion

Thank you for caring about developing yourself and your capabilities as a coach and for giving all that you do to the clients and organizations you support. Whether you specifically label them as such or not, many of the skills you employ in providing your coaching service are based on your own emotional and social intelligence. We are more effective in using our skills and in coaching others to develop theirs when we understand these emotional and social intelligence strategies, and when we can identify the particular ESE strategies benefiting or challenging our clients.

The value of this book will come to life when it assists you in gaining clarity about what emotions are motivating you to respond a certain way. Its value will be brought to bear when you work with your clients and organizations to expand their ESE awareness and capabilities.

As humans we can't act or think without using our emotions. That makes emotions an imperative part of the coaching domain. We aren't islands unto ourselves; we are social beings. Our social effectiveness is interwoven throughout all our coaching. Dr. Reuven Bar-On has pointed out that the same parts of our brain are activated when we work with our emotions as when we use our social capacities; these two fundamental human elements—our emotional and social capacities—should not, and really cannot, be separated.

After a very long time during which emotions have been considered a distraction or worse, the idea of measuring emotions is now taking hold and gaining traction. Finally, emotions are being consciously welcomed into our workplace, our community, and our individual lives. This has been influenced by the development of the scientifically credible emotional intelligence assessments we discuss in Chapter One. It has led Newfield Network to develop its Ontology of Emotions™, and, as Lee Salmon describes, it's guided NASA to be able to make increased sense of what happened with the O-ring failure in the Challenger shuttle disaster. Congratulations to NASA and so many other agencies and organizations who have taken dramatic steps to improve skills in communications and interpersonal empowerment. There have been powerful applications of emotional and social effectiveness. We know there are many successes yet to come, especially as you take your awareness and increased capabilities into your coaching practice.

We invite you to use this book actively as you enhance your skills in Coaching for Emotional Intelligence.

We wish you well! Enjoy and profit from further integrating emotional and social effectiveness into your coaching practice and your organizations.

# References

Bamberger, M., & Bradley, H. (2005, May). Leaders growing leaders: Using AI every day to deliver America's dream. *AI Practitioner: The International Journal of AI Best Practice*, pp. 22–25.

Bar-On, R. (1997). *The Emotional Quotient Inventory (EQ-i): Technical manual.* Toronto: Multi-Health Systems.

Bar-On, R. (2001). EI and self-actualization. In J. Ciarrochi, J. Forgas, & J. Mayer (Eds.), *Emotional intelligence in everyday life.* New York: Psychology Press.

Barsade, S. (2002). The ripple effect: Emotional contagion and its influence on group behavior. *Administrative Science Quarterly, 47,* 644–675.

Beck, D.E., & Cowan, C.C. (1996). *Spiral dynamics: Mastering values, leadership, and change.* Malden, MA: Blackwell.

Bharwaney, G. (2007). Coaching executives to enhance emotional intelligence and increase productivity. In R. Bar-On, J.G. Maree, & M.J. Elian (Eds.), *Educating people to be emotionally intelligent.* Westport, CT: Praeger.

Boyatzis, R.E. (2001). How and why individuals are able to develop emotional intelligence. In C. Cherniss & D. Goleman (Eds.), *The emotionally intelligent workplace.* San Francisco: Jossey-Bass.

Boyatzis, R.E. (2006). Core competencies in coaching others to overcome dysfunctional behavior. In V.U. Druskat, F. Sala, & G. Mount (Eds.), *Linking emotional intelligence and performance at work: Current research evidence with individuals and groups* Mahwah, NJ: Lawrence Erlbaum Associates.

Breakthrough ideas for tomorrow's business agenda. (2003, April). *Harvard Business Review.*

Brothers, C. (2004). *Language and the pursuit of happiness.* Naples, FL: New Possibilities Press.

Buckingham, M., & Coffman, C. (1999). *First break all the rules: What the world's greatest managers do differently*, New York: Simon & Schuster.

Burns, D. (1980). *Feeling good: The new mood therapy*. New York: Signet.

Carkhuff, R. (1971). *The development of human resources*. New York: Holt, Rinehart and Winston.

Cherniss, C., & Goleman, D. (2001). *The emotionally intelligent workplace*. San Francisco: Jossey-Bass.

CERA. (2006), *OCC Executive Coaching Program FY 07*. Washington, DC: U.S. Department of Treasury, Office of the Comptroller of the Currency.

dePalma, A. (2006, August 25). E.P.A. whistle-blower says U.S. hid 9/11 dust danger. *New York Times*.

Druskat, V.U., Sala, F., & Mount, G. (2006). *Linking emotional intelligence and performance at work*. Mahwah, NJ: Lawrence Erlbaum Associates.

Ekman, P. (2003). *Emotions revealed*. New York: Henry Holt and Company.

Federal Consulting Group. (2006). *OCC Treasury pilot coaching program evaluation report*. Washington, DC: U.S. Department of the Treasury.

Goleman, D. (1998). *Working with emotional intelligence*. New York: Bantam.

Gowing, M.K., O'Leary, B.S., Brienza, D., Cavallo, K., & Crain, R. (2006). A practitioner's research agenda: Exploring real-world applications and issues. In V.U. Druskat, F. Sala, & G. Mount (Eds.). *Linking emotional intelligence and performance at work: Current research evidence with individuals and groups.* Mahwah, NJ: Lawrence Erlbaum Associates.

Harman, W., & Sahtouris, E. (1998). *Biology revisioned*. Berkeley, CA: North Atlantic Books.

Hay/McBer Research and Innovation Group (1997). This research was provided to Daniel Goleman and is reported in his book (Goleman, 1998).

Hughes, M. (2006). *Life's 2% solution*. Boston: Nicholas Brealey.

Hughes, M., & Terrell, J.B. (2007). *The emotionally intelligent team*. San Francisco: Jossey-Bass.

Hughes, M., Patterson, L.B., & Terrell, J.B. (2005). *Emotional intelligence in action: Training and coaching activities for leaders and managers*. San Francisco: Pfeiffer.

Karlin, D. (2007, April). *Clerk of the Privy Counsel, Kevin Lynch: His viewpoint*. Paper presented at the ICCO Third Symposium, Washington, D.C.

Kennedy, J.F. (1957). *Profiles in courage*. New York: PocketBooks.

Lennick, D. (2007). Emotional competence development and the bottom line. In R. Bar-On, J.G. Maree, & M.J. Elian (Eds.), *Educating people to be emotionally intelligent*. Westport, CT: Praeger.

Lewis, T., Amini, F., & Lannon, R. (2000). *A general theory of love*. New York: Vintage.

Luskin, F., Aberman, R., & DeLorenzo, A. (2005). *The training of emotional competence in financial services advisors*. Article found at www.eiconsortium.org.

Maslow, A.H. (1943). A theory of human motivation. *Psychological Review, 50*, 370–396.

Maslow, A.H. (1976). *The farther reaches of human nature.* New York: Penguin Books.

Maturana, H., & Varela, F. (1987). *The tree of knowledge.* Boston: Shambhala Publications.

Mayer, J. D., & Salovey, P. (1997). What is emotional intelligence? In P. Salovey & D. Sluyter (Eds.), *Emotional development and emotional intelligence: Implications for educators.* New York: Basic Books.

Olalla, J. (1998). *The ritual side of coaching.* Boulder, CO: Newfield Network, Inc.

Olalla, J. (2004a). *From knowledge to wisdom.* Boulder, CO: Newfield Network, Inc.

Olalla, J. (2004b). Ontology of a leader. White Paper. Boulder, CO: Newfield Network, Inc.

O'Reilly, M. (2007, June 5). Personal conversation.

Partnership for Public Service. (2007). *Where the jobs are: Mission critical opportunities for America* (2nd ed.). Washington, DC: Author.

Pearce, J.C. (2000). *The biology of transcendence.* Rochester, VT: Park Street Press.

Pert, C. (1997). *The molecules of emotion.* New York: Simon & Schuster.

Plutchik, R. (2001) The nature of emotions. *American Scientist, 89,* 344–335.

Rath, T. (2006). *Vital friends: The people you can't afford to live without.* Washington, DC: Gallup Press.

Roberto, M.A. (2005). *Why great leaders don't take yes for an answer.* Upper Saddle River, NJ: Wharton School Publishing.

Rock, D., & Schwartz, J. (2006, Summer). The neuroscience of leadership. *Strategy and Business.* Available at www.strategy-business.com/press/freearticle/06207.

Ruderman, M.N., Hannum, K., Leslie, J.B., and Steed, J. (2001). *Leadership skills and emotional intelligence.* Colorado Springs, CO: Center for Creative Leadership.

Seligman, M.E.P. (1990). *Learned optimism.* New York: Knopf.

Seligman, M.E.P. (2002). *Authentic happiness.* New York: The Free Press.

Schlosser, B., Steinbrenner, D., Kumata, E., & Hunt, J. (2006). The coaching impact study: Measuring the value of executive coaching. *The International Journal of Coaching in Organizations, 3,* 8–26.

Speilberger, C. (Ed.). (2004). *Encyclopedia of applied psychology.* New York: Academic Press.

United States Government Accountability Office. (2006). Learning from the past and preparing for the future: Presentation by the Honorable David M. Walker, Comptroller General of the United States, GAO-06-1034CG. Washington, DC: U.S. Government Accountability Office.

Wangler, J. (2007). *The art of cultivating space to grow: Creative learning groups (CLGs) at NASA Goddard Space Flight Center.* Washington, DC: EDIN Associates.

Wheatley, M. (1994). *Leadership and the new science: Learning about organization from an orderly universe,* San Francisco: Berrett-Koehler.

Wheatley, M. (2002). *Turning to one another: Simple conversations to restore hope to the future.* San Francisco: Berrett-Koehler.

## WEBSITES

http://bmj.com/cgi/content/full/330/7495/802

http://mentalhealth.samhsa.gov/publications/allpubs/SMA01-3481/SMA01-
3481ch2.asp

www.eiconsortium.org/research/business_case_for_ei.htm.

www.prnewswire.co.uk/cgi/news/release?id=125380

# *Resources*

## AUTHORS' CONSULTING SERVICES

### Collaborative Growth

Marcia Hughes, President
James Terrell, Vice President
P.O. Box 17509
Golden, CO 80402
303.271.0021
contact@cgrowth.com
www.cgrowth.com
www.TheEmotionallyIntelligentTeam.com

### Newfield Network, Inc.

Julio Olalla, Founder and President
Terrie Lupberger, MCC, CEO
75 Manhattan Dr, Suite 1
Boulder, CO 80303
303.449.6117
info@newfieldnetwork.com
www.newfieldnetwork.com

### Federal Consulting Group, Department of Treasury

G. Lee Salmon, Executive Consultant and Coach
799 9th St., NW, Washington, DC, 20239
lee.salmon@bpd.treas.gov
www.fcg.gov

### Learning for Living

- G. Lee Salmon: glsalmon@cox.net

### Coaching Organizations

- Association of Coach Training Organizations (ACTO): www.acto1.org
- International Coach Federation (ICF): www.coachfederation.org
- International Consortium for Coaching in Organizations (ICCO): www.coachconsortium.org

### Assessments

Contact information for the some of the assessments identified in this book follows.

- **TESI®.** Collaborative Growth®, P.O. Box 17509, Golden, CO 80402, contact@cgrowth.com, www.TheEmotionallyIntelligentTeam.com; www.cgrowth.com.
- **Bar-On EQ-i®, Leadership Report, EQ-360®, The Benchmark of Organizational Emotional Intelligence (BOEI), MSCEIT®.** Multi-Health Systems, Inc. P.O. Box 950, North Tonawanda, NY 14120-0950, 800.456.3003; customerservice@mhs.com, www.mhs.com
- **ECI 360.** EI Hay Group, 877-267-8375. http://ei.haygroup.com
- **Emergenetics.** Emergenetics International, 2 Inverness Dr East, Suite 189, Englewood, CO 80112, (303) 660-7920. www.emergenetics.com

## RESEARCH IN EMOTIONAL INTELLIGENCE

**EI Consortium.** The Consortium for Research on Emotional Intelligence in Organizations aids the advancement of research and practice related to emotional intelligence in organizations. www.eiconsortium.org.

# *Index*

# About the Authors

**James Bradford Terrell** is vice president of Collaborative Growth®, L.L.C., where he applies his expertise in interpersonal communication to help a variety of public and private sector clients anticipate change and respond to it resiliently.

Co-author of *Coaching for Emotional Intelligence* (2008), *The Emotionally Intelligent Team* (2007), and *Emotional Intelligence in Action (2005),* he coaches leaders, teams in transition, and senior management, using the Bar-On EQi®, EQ 360®, and other assessments. James provides train-the-trainer workshops and educates coaches on how to develop insightful interpretation and application of EQ results. He also works as a consultant and contract mediator for the U.S. Forest Service and other federal agencies.

James worked as a psychotherapist in private practice for many years and served as executive director of the Syntropy Institute, a not-for-profit research organization investigating how communication training impacts human effectiveness. He also served as the director of training for the Metro-Denver Mutual Housing Association, an early developer of cooperative housing in the Denver area.

In a previous life, he was the owner/operator of Integrity Building Systems, a construction company specializing in residential and commercial renovation and served as a project coordinator on a wide variety of building projects including

Denver International Airport and the National Digital Cable Television Center. In a future life he is certain he will be a rock star.

**Marcia Hughes** is president of Collaborative Growth®, L.L.C., and serves as a strategic communications partner for teams and their leaders in organizations that value high performers. She weaves her expertise in emotional intelligence throughout her consulting work, facilitation, team building, and workshops to help people motivate themselves and communicate more effectively with others. Her keynotes are built around powerful stories of how success can grow when people work collaboratively. Businesses, government agencies, and nonprofits have all benefited in such areas as team and leadership development, strategic design, and conflict resolution from her proven formula for success. She is co-author of *Coaching for Emotional Intelligence* (2008), *The Emotionally Intelligent Team* (2007), *Emotional Intelligence in Action (2005)*, and author of *Life's 2% Solution.*

Marcia is a certified trainer in the Bar-On EQ-i and EQ 360. She provides train-the-trainer training and coaching in powerful EQ delivery. Her efforts to improve productivity in the workplace through strategic communication grew out of a distinguished career in law, where her firm specialized in complex public policy matters. There again, her leadership and communication skills enabled Hughes's team to effectively address controversial environmental, land use, and water development matters involving numerous stakeholders, which included federal, state, and local governments, along with the general public.

As an assistant attorney general, she served the Department of Public Health and the Environment. She clerked on the 10th Circuit Court of Appeals for the Honorable William E. Doyle.

## CONTRIBUTING CO-AUTHORS

**Julio Olalla** is an internationally renowned educator and speaker, known for his passion and dedication to creating new paradigms of *learning* for the sake of addressing the global, complex issues we are facing today. Julio is considered one of the founders of the profession of coaching and is known for his ability to create supportive and empowering learning environments for individuals and organizations to explore *new* thinking. He is the founder and president of the Newfield Network, an international education, coaching, and consulting company with headquarters in the United States, Chile, and Europe.

For more than twenty-two years, Julio has worked directly with thousands of people in over ten different countries teaching over 50,000 individuals in leadership, executive coaching, and building trust. He creates a space of such safety, trust, and respect that individuals and teams are able to work their deepest concerns in his programs.

For more information, visit www.newfieldnetwork.com or contact him at julio@newfieldnetwork.com

**Terrie Lupberger** is CEO of the Newfield Network, Inc., an international learning and executive coaching company. Terrie, a Master Certified Coach, specializes in coaching women in leadership positions. She is also a faculty member in the Certified Financial Coach™ training programs taught around the country that aim to increase both emotional intelligence and financial savvy in individuals.

Terrie's earlier career was spent working in two federal agencies for more than fourteen years. At the Department of the Treasury, she was a senior financial systems analyst and later worked with the U.S. Courts to help improve the operations of the federal court system.

One of Terrie's passions is working with organizational leaders and teams to help them increase their emotional effectiveness and capacity to generate more successful and sustainable futures.

For more information visit www.newfieldnetwork.com or contact her at terrie.lupberger@newfieldnetwork.com.

**G. Lee Salmon** is the practice leader for executive coaching, mentoring, and leadership development with the Federal Consulting Group, U.S. Department of Treasury. Lee is an executive consultant, certified executive coach with the International Coach Federation, and has more than forty years of leadership and management experience working in the public and private sectors.

For the past twelve years, Lee has coached political appointees, executives, and senior managers in the executive branch of the federal government. He also has a private coaching practice, Learning for Living, where he works with executives in the private sector. He has degrees and certificates in physics, change management, and leadership development and specializes in working with scientific and technical organizations. Currently he is on the board of directors for the International Consortium of Coaching in Organizations and is the author of numerous articles and publications on coaching and leadership.

When Geoffrey, her coach, first met Bridget, he found her quite pleasant; however, he was a bit concerned that she seemed to be entering into coaching with minor curiosity, but little passion. She was charming and appeared to be willing to be candid, especially about what she considered her faults to be, but she seemed only moderately invested in making this a growth opportunity. She laughed and said she was bad at doing homework so if he had any she'd give it a try, but he shouldn't count on it.

Bridget indicated she'd recently taken two emotional intelligence questionnaires, the EQ-i® and the EQ 360® in which her boss, direct reports, and peers rated her. Her scores bothered her; she was surprised they were so low. So she saw this coaching as the chance to improve her emotional intelligence. The coaching program design included several meetings in which her supervisor joined them in the coaching session to provide feedback, organizational perspective, and support. While at times a manager's involvement can hinder frankness, in this case it worked well. Bridget and her boss have a positive and trusting relationship. As a matter of fact, her boss had more ambition for her than she did. He seemed to want more out of the coaching process than Bridget was ready for.

Bridget said she only had one goal for the coaching: She would really like to expand her emotional awareness. Her manager, on the other hand, wanted her to improve her positioning so she'd gain more face time with the senior leadership and get a promotion soon. Geoffrey sensed that once he and Bridget had a chance to explore things more openly in coaching sessions that her real interests were likely to unfold with greater clarity and might possibly change considerably. She just needed the chance to access a more trusting and introspective state. The boss's suggestions were relevant, but not controlling of their process.

They worked together for six months, and began by reviewing results from several assessments Bridget had taken over the last year. Geoffrey also asked her to fully describe her current situation as a whole person—on and off work. He invited her to talk about what worked, what didn't work, when she felt challenged, and when she felt strong. Without trying to fix anything, they took time to discover a clear sense of where Bridget wasn't as satisfied with her life as she wanted and felt some real passion to improve. At first her passion was carefully veiled because she believed her life functioned just fine, and she wasn't about to upset the apple cart. She seemed to carefully control how much emotional energy she exhibited.

Geoffrey didn't accept or reject her limited scope for the coaching; rather he asked her to wait until the second session to even start exploring the possible learning goals for their relationship. He said taking more time would facilitate a fresh spirit of inquiry and open learning. Bridget was intrigued. Problem solving was her career, and she was good at it, but now that the "problem" to be fixed had been left open, her inquiring mind began to start noticing parts of her life that she hadn't been noticing. She told her coach about her team, how they were a fairly new division and worked okay together, but she often felt many didn't respect her as their boss. It seemed more like they thought of her as staff right along with them. In response to Geoffrey's questions about how she felt about it, Bridget seemed surprised to begin recognizing her frustration, but she was cautious to make sure her concern didn't get too big. She wanted to stay in control. Geoffrey was beginning to wonder whether they might be working on the ESE skill of valuing self, but he knew he needed to learn more before deciding.

She described the limited access she had to the senior team and her lack of energy about a promotion. She would be happy with one, but. . . . She couldn't put her finger on why it didn't seem exciting, but it didn't. She didn't indicate any fear, just no passion.

Then she talked about her husband and three children. All of a sudden the picture filled out considerably! She had a teenager in high school getting ready for college, one in middle school, and one in elementary school. She and her husband had very demanding professional jobs and didn't believe in getting any more child care help than they really had to. They wanted to be the ones to help their children face their challenges and develop the skills for coping with life. Now Bridget came to life with passion, angst, and funny stories. She started asking for advice on how to coach her ten-year-old perfectionist daughter to lighten up. She wondered how to give the right amount of advice to her high school son so she'd be there for him, but not overdo it. Suddenly, there was traction.

Bridget and Geoffrey found that her EQ-i scores were important indicators of her family challenges as well as work challenges. Bridget had not developed any patterns of paying attention to her own emotions. She knew she cared a lot about issues with her team, but often would take a long time